Ghosts and L
of Nottinghamshire

David Haslam

COUNTRYSIDE BOOKS

NEWBURY, BERKSHIRE

First published 1996
© David Haslam 1996

COUNTRYSIDE BOOKS
3 Catherine Road
Newbury, Berkshire

ISBN 185306 429 7

*In memory of Alfred J. Perkins
(1922–1996) a dear friend and
neighbour sadly missed.*

Map by Trevor Yorke
Cover illustration by Colin Doggett
Designed by Mon Mohan

Produced through MRM Associates Ltd., Reading
Typeset by Textype, Cambridge
Printed by J. W. Arrowsmith Ltd., Bristol

Acknowledgements

I would like to thank the following people for their contribution to this book. My thanks go to all those people who agreed to share their experiences and whose words and recollections appear in the book; to the local historians and authors who gave me advice and permission to quote from their own works; special thanks to Captain Roy Peters, Mr David Bradbury and Mr Roy Waggott; to the editors of those local newspapers who gave me permission to quote from their pages; to the staffs of the county's library and archives service for their unfailing courtesy and thorough professionalism; and finally my special thanks go to Mrs Barbara Thomson and Mrs Margaret Davies for their proof reading and for editorial suggestions.

Ghosts and Legends of Nottinghamshire

Introduction

NOTTINGHAMSHIRE is a county of contrasts; farms and forest, factories and mines, bustling urban centres and historic market towns all combine to form its character and history. The county is undergoing something of a post-industrial 'greening'. Some of the rural ex-pit villages are becoming the sleepy backwaters they were prior to the pits. Tourism is a growth industry as visitors from around the world come to sample the varied charms the county has to offer. Nottinghamshire is 'Robin Hood Country' and Sherwood Forest, the county's greatest natural attraction, is being enhanced and extended by a variety of local initiatives.

There are more ghosts in this book than legends, and some folk tales, such as the Miller of Mansfield and the Wise Men of Gotham, do not appear here. This is either because they have been dealt with by other writers, notably Polly Howat in *Tales of Old Nottinghamshire*, or because they are simply not to my taste. Some legends, like that of Robin Hood, must be tackled by anyone writing about Nottinghamshire. There are a plethora of books, both non-fiction and fiction, that deal with Robin. However, there is no one primary source or tradition upon which to draw. I have not retold the Robin Hood stories in this book, but I have attempted to dig beneath the legends as they have evolved and reconcile them with local folklore, place-name evidence and local history. There is a section devoted to him, and he makes an appearance in many of the items on individual places. Readers may be left unsatisfied; if so they should begin their own quest for Robin Hood.

The accounts of ghosts are of two kinds – the first hand accounts of people I have interviewed and tape recorded and those from secondary sources such as archives and newspapers. With some of the older ghost stories there are no modern reports of these ghosts being seen. This suggests that ghosts, like memories, fade with time. To quote from Byron's *Don Juan*:

Coin'd from surviving Superstition's mint,
Which passes ghosts in currency like gold,
But rarely seen, like gold compared with paper.

Those accounts I have gathered first hand I have tried to present in as straightforward a way as possible. I am convinced that the people I have interviewed genuinely experienced the events they have described to me. The exact nature of that experience I leave for readers to decide for themselves. As evidence for the existence of ghosts such first hand accounts are very much like hearsay evidence given in legal testimony. Despite the hours of painstaking efforts by hundreds of researchers no scientific proof for ghosts exists. However, science, in the light of the extraordinary experiences of ordinary people, cannot provide all the answers. Ghosts are one enigma of many, a part of the human experience that makes us question our understanding of the universe. This is central to the appeal of 'The Unexplained' – it gives us back our sense of wonder.

The first book that really gripped me was a book of ghost stories, and I read it in Sherwood Forest. I was a boy scout and my troop was at the scout camp at Walesby. I bought the collection for next to nothing at a jumble sale, and my friends teased me about having my nose stuck in a book. It was a very different matter when, at night in the big old army tent, I read aloud ghost stories by torchlight. In the gloom I could see them around me, transfixed, wide eyes shining in the dark. I have been fascinated by ghosts and folklore ever since. This book then is a settling of accounts with the boy that was. I have sought out the ghosts and legends of Nottinghamshire so that others, hopefully, will be as entertained and fascinated in their recounting as I have been in their retelling.

David Haslam

ARNOLD

The Leisure Centre Phantom

THE Bonnington Theatre is part of Arnold Leisure Centre complex, which opened in 1982. Many of the staff believe the theatre is haunted. Ghostly footsteps have been heard in the empty building at night. A chilling presence has been felt on the landing leading into the theatre and in the lighting box upstairs on the floor above. According to Mrs Lynda Jordan, the Centre Manager, 'Lots of staff have had odd experiences here, even new staff who don't know about the ghost. Some staff are not keen to go up to the theatre at all. When they have to lock up the building they never ever go up to the theatre alone.

'One leisure attendant knew that the lights in the theatre were switched off and went through to put them on. He had to unlock a door to get to the switches. When he got to them the lights were switched on already. There is no way that any one else could have got into the lighting box, there was only one key and he had it. He was a bit surprised, but came out and locked the door behind him. When he got downstairs one of the staff said to him, "I thought you'd gone up there to put the lights on!" The lights had been switched off again. He went back upstairs, unlocked the door and immediately felt that someone was in the lighting box. There was a strange, heavy perfume in the air. There was no one else there at all. He switched the lights on again. All the hairs on the back of his neck stood up. He ran down the stairs, jumped the last flight and nearly crashed into a glass trophy cabinet. I was downstairs on reception. I said, "Whatever are you doing?" He told me what had happened. I said, "You just can't leave it, you've got to go back up and look. Come on, I'll come with you." There was no one there and the lights were off. They had now been switched on, off, on, off and it was very cold up there. Bear in mind this building is usually very warm, with the pool downstairs being heated.

'Two clairvoyants have independently confirmed there

is a ghost here. A well-known Nottingham clairvoyant was at the centre with a group that used to use the facilities. She said that there was a presence in the toilets on the landing. She contacted her spirit guide to find out more. She said that the presence was female, and harmless, just a resident spirit. A gentleman clairvoyant booked the theatre from London to do a talk and an open evening. When he arrived we went into the theatre to get things ready. As soon as we came into the theatre he asked me if I knew that there was a presence here already. I said yes we did, as long as you don't have to lock up on your own it's all right, we were quite used to the idea by now.'

Why the ghost haunts the theatre remains unknown. There is some evidence to suggest that the leisure centre is built on, or near to, a Quaker burial ground. A letter dated 28th February 1717 from Nathaniel Need, a Quaker from Pennsylvania, said that his brother John 'was not to hinder friends of the privillage of the small burieing place near my house in Arnall.' It is documented that on 12th July 1725 a building for religious worship at a schoolhouse in Jackson's Yard, Arnold, was certified in the name of Joseph Need. This site is adjacent to the Arnold Leisure Centre. During the building work for the leisure centre bones and a skull were unearthed – were these from the Quaker cemetery?

BOUGHTON

The Ghost Factory

ALBERT and Sue Ilett lived in a house that was built on the site of an old brickworks. They were regularly woken at 6.30 am by a sound like that of two bricks being banged together. Though the factory was long gone the clatter of activity apparently remained: 'Sometimes we'd be laid in bed first thing in the morning and we'd hear this sound, like a chinking noise, as if someone were breaking bricks, or someone testing the bricks' hardness and soundness after firing. We would also hear this noise like boulders being rolled. I often got up and looked out to see where the sounds were coming from. It sometimes sounded as if my daughter were rolling marbles along her window sill, but whenever I looked she'd always be asleep. It was a real mystery, we lived with this for years.'

CARLTON-IN-LINDRICK

Signs and Wonders and the End of the World

FOLLOWING the Reformation, most English people adhered to the Anglican Church, the state religion. Others saw Anglicanism as too similar to the Roman Catholicism it had sought to replace. A multitude of dissenting churches sprang up. By the 17th century the 'dissenters', popularly called 'the Puritans', had become a vocal and influential minority, in business, the law, and in Parliament. The social tensions generated by economic change, between the state and religion, between Parliament and the Crown, finally erupted into civil war. Both the Royalists and Parliament claimed 'God on their side'. For some Puritans the war was seen in biblical terms, as the final conflict between good and evil; it was literally Armageddon, 'the End of the World'. It is against this backdrop, in the prelude to the English Civil War, that the following strange episode occurred.

'In the midst of life we are in death', yet sudden, unnatural death is always a traumatic event. Imagine then the shock to the village community of Carlton-in-Lindrick, when in 1641 a double tragedy claimed the lives of two bridesmaids, just days after a wedding. At that time Carlton was a quiet, rural backwater, with the villagers mostly working on the land. A visit to the market at nearby Worksop would have been quite an excursion for them.

Murder would have been a rare thing for this community. Consider then how the grief in the village would have turned into incredulity when one of the victims apparently came back to life, with a message from God that 'the end of the world was nigh'. This story comes via an old newspaper report on a 17th-century pamphlet that must have been the 'best-seller' of its day.

On the 12th November 1641 the wedding of James Turner, 'an honest townsman of Carlton', and Margaret Holbeck, daughter of Thomas Holbeck, deceased, of Blyth, took place at St Giles' church, Carlton-in-Lindrick. James had been servant and clerk to Sir Francis Thorney, who attended the wedding and provided the wedding feast. Bridesmaids to Margaret were James' 16 year old sister Jane and her best friend Hannah, daughter of one Simon Franklin of Worksop.

The wedding was a great success, thanks to the generosity of Sir Francis, both James and Margaret's families being of modest means. Despite this, James had provided his sister with a very expensive 'silk upper body' for her dress, of which the girl was understandably proud.

Four days later, on the 16th November 1641, both Jane Turner and Hannah Franklin were found dead. The pamphlet of 1642 says, 'Their sudden death brought great terror and fear upon the people: insomuch that someone thought them to be poisoned.' Was it murder? No motive for poisoning the two girls could be found. A suicide pact? No reason could be found, other than what seemed to be a girlish quarrel.

The day after the wedding the two bridesmaids visited the bride. At the girls' request Margaret introduced them to the daughter of Sir Francis Thorney, Mistress Anne. Jane Turner had again worn the 'silk upper body' her brother had given her. She wanted Mistress Anne to notice her fine clothes and turned the conversation to fashion. Anne Thorney, noting the girl's ill concealed delight in her new dress, remarked, 'Can thy father clothe thee thus and seem so poor?' Miss Turner took this to heart, but she said nothing and the girls finished their cakes and wine. It was only when her friend Hannah also began teasing her, boasting of her own dresses and finery in a way calculated to rekindle her jealousy, that Jane burst into tears and left the room. Did this event so upset Jane Turner that she poisoned her best friend, who had taunted her, and then poisoned herself? In the midst of such speculation, events took a bizarre turn.

In spite of their grief the families had to think about practicalities. One grave for both the girls at the Carlton churchyard was proposed. However, Mr Franklin, understandably, wanted his daughter buried at Worksop. This delayed the interments while separate funerals were arranged. With the grave ready at Carlton, Jane's mother came to view the corpse one last time. The pamphlet tells us that, as she lifted the shroud, 'Her daughter, even as one waking from slumber, raised up herself, and with a mild and cheerful countenance, spoke unto her mother as follows: My most dear mother, why have you sinned so sore against God? You have made me sorrowful many times, but be you content for God has forgiven all, for I am sent as a messenger unto you, and within five days I shall return to the place I came from, where I shall live in all peace.'

Jane Turner had been 'dead' for 20 hours. After getting up, dressing and eating she began to 'preach and speak prophesies'. News of the 'Maid of Carlton' spread quickly. Huge crowds gathered to hear the girl declaim from the window of her parents' house. This continued for five days and nights without her once sleeping or even lying down.

According to the pamphlet, the prophesies were 'many and singular', and she 'admonished all to repent of their sins for the end of the world is at hand'. In the midst of such dire news it seems her tormentor was not forgotten. The girl apparently foretold, 'the very clothes Mistress Anne did wear for her pride shall become loathsome to all people, whereby none shall be able to wear them'. The pamphlet tells that Anne's clothes developed a horrible smell, 'By reason of an evil savour about them,' that would not wash out and all of them had to be burnt. On the 20th of November Jane Turner collapsed and died, this time for good.

No explanation for this curious tale has been found and the truth may never be known. The 17th century was a traumatic time of war and religious persecution. North Nottinghamshire was a hotbed of sectarian fervour. The 'pilgrim fathers', whose religious zeal took them to the 'New World' in America, came from Scrooby, not far from Carlton-in-Lindrick. In *Tales of Witchcraft and Sorcery*, Ken Radford estimates that, between the 14th and 17th centuries, upwards of half a million people, mostly innocent women, were executed on this indictment. The effects of this mass delusion were seen in the witch trails at Salem, Massachusetts, in 1692. Twenty people died on the gallows on the evidence of the hysterical outbursts of some teenage girls. Can the events at Carlton-in-Lindrick be seen as a similar example of mass hysteria? Whatever the case, thanks to an anonymous 17th-century pamphleteer, the 'Maid of Carlton' has not been forgotten.

CALVERTON

The Lost Haunted House

LIKE the vicarage at Warsop, Calverton's Georgian vicarage was pulled down in the name of progress. Formerly the home of the Seely family, it became the vicar's house in 1912. Locally it had a reputation for being haunted. The last vicar to live there, the Rev Thomas Hoyle, told the press, 'Many people in the old village claim they saw a ghost in the old vicarage.' Over the years there had been much speculation about the village's haunted house. One villager claimed to have seen what seemed to be the ghost of an old lady disappear in front of him near the entrance to the grounds. Similarly, local youths talked about having seen an apparition at the same spot. It was said that dogs and horses were loath to pass the vicarage. Another villager noted that dogs shied away from the boundary wall near the gate. There were dark rumours about the vicarage's past. One held that the mother-in-law of a former vicar had hanged herself there. Another told that a servant girl had cut her own throat when jilted by the coachman. The vicar's wife, *Mrs Muriel Hoyle,* told a local newspaper, 'Ever since I first saw the place . . . I thought it eerie and foreboding.'

In common with many large country houses, this once elegant mansion fell into disrepair. To make way for the new miners' welfare hall the vicarage was scheduled to be demolished. The demolition crew came from Derbyshire and started work in late October 1961. However, it wasn't long before their task was interrupted. The foreman, Mr Wally Davis of Ripley, described what happened: 'We heard doors slamming shut long after the doors had been removed and a voice that can't be accounted for.'

In the second week of work Mr Davis and another member of the crew, Mr Ivan Holmes of Codnor, were sitting in a downstairs room waiting for a lift to their lodgings. Mr Davis told reporters, 'It was dark and the others had gone, when we heard a shuffling noise in an upstairs room.' Their initial response was that another workman had returned to gather firewood. They called but they got no answer. Then a door upstairs slammed and the shuffling noise continued. The two men became concerned for the safety of whoever was upstairs as by now the upper storey was partially demolished and almost all of the floorboards had been ripped up. They decided to investigate. Mr Davis went up the main staircase and Mr Holmes went up by the back stairs, hoping to intercept the intruder between them. They met nobody and proceeded to search the upper storey. The noises were coming from one room in particular, a converted bathroom. As they approached the room both men were startled by the sudden, violent crash of breaking crockery. This continued for some time, only to stop as suddenly as it had started. As this room had most of its floor missing neither man was keen to venture any further and they both went downstairs. They were left with two mysteries – who was smashing the crockery, and where, in an empty house under demolition, had the crockery come from?

Speaking afterwards, Mr Holmes said, 'We just don't know what to make of it. I have never given such things much attention before, but it was a very peculiar experience.' When asked for his comment the Rev Hoyle said, 'I think it would be very rash to say outright that there is nothing in it.' The demolition was completed as planned, but what became of the ghost or ghosts? Certainly no further reports of weird happenings on the site of the old vicarage have appeared. Has the ghost found a new haunt, or were the events of November 1961 its last appearance?

CHILWELL

The Ghost of a Murdered Peddler

IN the 19th century Chilwell was a village; now it is all but an indistinguishable part of Nottingham's urban sprawl. In 1850, however, it became briefly famous. Newspaper reports appeared across the country that for years a cottage had been made uninhabitable by a ghost that had become the dread of the villagers.

John Baguley lay dying in the February of that year. On his deathbed he made a confession that some 25 years earlier he had murdered a peddler who lived at the cottage. With the imminent prospect of 'meeting his maker', Baguley told the whole story. He had killed the man for two reasons, his cottage, which Baguley later sold, and because the peddler and Baguley's daughter were sweethearts. Baguley was set against the match, and the peddler's death would free his daughter for a better prospect. Whether Baguley got a son-in-law he approved of is unrecorded but the profit from the cottage brought him little comfort. Local talk of the 'Chilwell Ghost' was a constant reminder of his crime. Remorse and guilt ate away at John Baguley's heart for 25 years until he died aged 70.

CLIPSTONE

The Poltergeist at the Dog and Duck

THE Dog and Duck pub at Clipstone was originally a farmhouse. The building dates from about 1821 and it probably became a pub to serve the needs of those travelling and working on the nearby railway branch line to Mansfield. Clipstone itself is an old village, mentioned in the Domesday Book. From the pub you can see the ruins of 'King John's Palace', once a magnificent Royal hunting lodge. It was built in the middle of the 12th century by Henry II. King John is likely to have held his parliament of 1212 here rather than under the 'Parliament Oak' in Sherwood. Edward I also held parliament at Clipstone in 1290. It was used by every English king that visited Sherwood to hunt the royal deer until the 15th century when it fell into disuse. The ruins that can still be seen today are part of the undercroft of a chamber and chapel built by Edward I in 1279. According Mr S. Jackson Coleman, in his book *Quaint Lore of Nottinghamshire*, the ruins are haunted by the ghost of an old lady in black. Folklore also has it that Robin Hood first met Maid Marian, the ward of King John, when he ambushed her party on their way to the 'palace'. After some dalliance in the woods Marian was returned to her guardian, having lost her heart to Robin.

When Mike Colman and his wife Marie arrived at the pub in December 1993 it came as little surprise to them that the Dog and Duck was haunted. Two of their previous pubs had ghosts. In Mike's words, 'I am not sure if the ghosts follow us, or we follow the ghosts! We hadn't been here all that long, and we didn't know about this pub being haunted. It was a Saturday night and I was just on my way out, when I was called to change a barrel of mild. I went belting down the cellar and just as I got to the top of the cellar steps I saw something sort of flash in front of me. So quick, just a blur. All the hairs on my neck stood up. I belted down the steps after it, but there was nothing there.

The hairs on my neck were still standing up. I thought, "Hello here we go again." I knew it was something funny. A couple of days before that Marie had been upstairs doing the ironing. She felt as if someone was watching her and she thought she had seen someone out of the corner of her eye the other side of the room.

'Later that same Saturday night, we were here about midnight having a late drink, there were about a dozen of us. In the kitchen all the pots and pans that are hanging up started to bang. Clang, clang, clang, they went. We went in there and all the pans were swinging. We all heard and saw it. We've had the pots and pans clanging in the kitchen any number of times since.

'The following Saturday the same people were here after hours and we heard this gushing sound. We went into the kitchen and the cold water tap was full on. I kept turning it, but couldn't turn the thing off. I went down into the cellar to turn it off on the mains. I tried to get a plumber the next day, it was Sunday and we had no water. The emergency plumber came about lunchtime and he showed me the washer. It was absolutely shredded. He said, "Have you had any trouble with this tap?" I said none at all. "Well," he said, "I've never seen one like that, it is so shredded, as if someone has been turning the tap tighter and tighter. Very unusual."

'We've also had loud thumps from the cellar. We've heard them from up here, just like a barrel tipping over or being dropped. I've been down to investigate, but nothing has fallen down or been shifted. One of our staff, Ben, was getting changed near the cellar door. I was standing next to him and it went again, a real big thump. I looked at him and all the colour had drained from his face. "Are you coming down?" I said. "No way," said Ben. Again everything was as it should be in the cellar, nothing had shifted. We have also had the burglar alarm go off in the family dining area three or four times in the middle of the night. Always at the same time, three o'clock in the morning. The first time it went off, I came down with a poker, there was no one there. The second time I thought it was a fault, so we had it checked, it was fine, and it still went off another twice.

16

'All this happened in the first two or three months of us arriving here. We've had one really big thump, and it's all settled down since. Having said that, the video remote control has absolutely disappeared. It cost £42 for a new control, so we searched very diligently. My passport went missing, we found it again in an odd place. This is funny because the same thing happened at my other pub just before a holiday. My passport is always kept in a file. This time it was behind some books on the bookshelf. Somewhere where no one would put it.'

In conversations with regulars and the previous landlord, Mike has learnt something of the pub's past. According to one local whose forebears worked on the farm before it became a pub, several people had died there, which is not surprising in an old building. The general opinion is there is a ghost at the top of the stairs leading to the landlord's accommodation, another in the main bedroom, and definitely something in the cellar. No one seems to know anything about the cause of the clanging pots and pans in the kitchen.

Mike has never seen anything ghostly in the pub, apart from the occasional distraction out of the corner of his eye, but he knows someone who has: 'Eric, who works here, did holiday relief for the previous landlord and he slept in the front bedroom. He told me that one night he woke up in bed to see a figure walking through the wall, coming towards him. He nudged his wife, but by the time she woke up, the figure had melted away. He was terrified, but next day he felt that this wouldn't stop him sleeping there again. One or two landlords are said to have died in that room.'

Mike compared his experiences at the Dog and Duck with those of two of his previous pubs, one in Nottingham and the other in Derby. The Thurland pub in Nottingham is built on the site of Thurland Hall. Incidents at the Thurland were very similar to those at Clipstone. However, Mike told me that the events at the Dog and Duck weren't a patch on the happenings at the pub he kept in Derby, the Green Man. This pub dates back to 1642 and was built next to an ancient graveyard. The Green Man had a resident ghost, called 'George' by the regulars. Mike saw George once, one Sunday evening, leaning against the piano. Footsteps were often heard upstairs when everyone was downstairs. One bedroom defied all attempts to warm it up, and the family dog refused to enter it.

Mike recalled, 'Things really got out of hand when workmen discovered several bodies buried beneath the pub's toilets. "We've found George," said the foreman. There were four bodies, two adults, a child and a dog. They were later identified as Saxon remains by Nottingham University. From the first evening after the bodies were unearthed the atmosphere in the pub changed. Lights switched on and off without cause, the piano was moved by unseen hands, bumps and bangs disturbed the night, and the fruit machine played itself. In one incident a grillpan for a toasted sandwich maker crashed to the floor behind the bar. Startled customers then watched the pan zoom across the floor. The pub emptied of customers within minutes! After the bodies were given Christian burial the disturbances ceased. The Green Man was frightening, the Dog and Duck is mild by comparison.'

Ghostly Maids at Archway House

ARCHWAY HOUSE, Clipstone, is a folly built by the Duke of Portland, based on the 12th-century Priory Gatehouse at Worksop. The house itself is set well back from the road, about a mile along a rutted bridlepath. Standing alone amidst a variety of mature trees, Archway House is an impressive sight. I was lucky enough to catch one of the owners in her garden. I learnt from her that a group of like minded people had come to the house about 15 years ago, seeking rural tranquillity, and had been at work restoring the property ever since. It now provides a fine country residence for several families. Local folklore has it, however, that Archway House is haunted.

The lady I spoke to confirmed that there were ghosts in Archway House, but for her 'It's not a problem.' She recalled that a psychic friend of hers had felt that there were several presences here, possibly servants or maids.

This was confirmed by her husband who, whilst washing up one night, saw a spectral figure pass through the kitchen, walking through the door and out into the night. Being dressed for bed he didn't follow. However, there was snow on the ground outside and, looking through the kitchen window after the retreating figure, he could clearly see that it left no footprints. The lady resident reiterated that the ghosts are very much part of the house and its character. The occupiers of Archway House live in harmony with their ghosts, indeed as they are trying to do with the beautiful countryside that surrounds them. Anyone using the bridlepath or looking at the house should respect the residents' privacy and peaceful life.

CODDINGTON

Godson's Ghost

MOST of those who could have shed light on the story of Godson's Ghost are dead. Why it should haunt a 17th-century cottage in Coddington, near Newark, is a mystery. The ghost is said to have been there for almost 200 years. The cottage was owned by several generations of the Godson family, and no doubt many family members were born and died there. The only surviving member of the Godsons is Mrs Joyce Golland, whose grandmother was the last of the family to live at the cottage. Mrs Golland remembers that both her mother and grandmother spoke about an unnatural chill and eerie presence in the downstairs front room, and at times both were afraid to go in there on their own. She also remembers that the neighbours living in the farmhouse opposite spoke of seeing lights at the windows at night, when it was known that all the Godsons were away, and that a visitor to the house once complained that something had shaken their bed the night before.

The cottage has been in the possession of the Wright family since the 1940s and it was renamed 'Windrome Cottage' after the nearby Winthorpe Aerodrome. The present owner, Mr J. Wright, inherited the house from his father, who in turn had it from his. In the Wright family the presence of Godson's Ghost was always noted and joked about when things were lost or misplaced. In 1973 Mr Wright's maternal grandmother died in the cottage. Joyce, now Mrs Golland, returned there to help prepare the food whilst the family were at the funeral. She experienced a most eerie feeling that there was an unseen presence in the cottage and that it was watching her.

For many years Mr Wright regarded Godson's Ghost as a piece of folklore, that is until one November night around 1983. He was returning home from spending a quiet hour at the Lord Nelson pub at Winthorpe. It was about 9.30 when he reached the cottage and he was quite sober. 'I had just walked in through our gateway and, rather than walk up the drive, I took a short cut across the lawn. Suddenly I was aware of someone walking up the drive parallel to me. I turned and looked and I could see this dark silhouette of a small figure. My first thought was that it could have been my mother returning to the house having put out the empty milk bottles. I said "Hello, who is it?" There was no reply. I thought we might have an intruder, so I walked swiftly to our front door and reached inside to switch the outside light on. To my dismay there was no one there. It was as if whoever it was had disappeared into thin air. When I finally went inside the house I found my mother watching TV. She hadn't been out of the house all evening. Feeling somewhat disconcerted by all of this, I fetched a torch and went to look around the house and outbuildings. There was no sign of anyone there. For quite some time after this I was rather reluctant to go outside at night.'

There have been no reports of anything unusual happening at the cottage of late. However, it seems unlikely that the last has been heard of Godson's Ghost.

COLSTON BASSETT

The Tunnel Ghost and a Spectral Congregation

IN medieval times Colston Bassett was made prosperous by the wool trade, but changes in agriculture and the drift of country people into the towns has left the village a quieter place than it once was. The fine manor house of the Golding family is sadly gone, but the underground passage that linked it to a Roman Catholic chapel is said to remain hidden to this very day. The tunnel is thought to be haunted by a priest who starved to death down there. He was hidden and forgotten about, all assuming he had made his escape when actually a lingering and tormented end befell him. His anguished moans are still heard coming from deep underground.

St Mary's church dates back to Norman times and had to be expanded in Colston Bassett's boom years. At its greatest extent it had two aisles and a south transept. However, gradual depopulation of the village meant that by the 18th century St Mary's was too big and its upkeep too much for the congregation. The north aisle was demolished and by the 19th century the church was in such disrepair that it was closed and replaced by a new one, St John the Divine. To prevent St Mary's being put to some profane use, the church authorities removed the roof and so hastened its decline. However, local people have heard the bells of St Mary's ringing, although removed long ago. Hymn singing and the responses of a long dead congregation at prayer have also been known to come from the church. Strange lights have been seen there at night, but their cause remains a mystery.

COLWICK

White Lady of Colwick

ACCORDING to local tradition, the White Lady of Colwick haunts Colwick Park. During the Reform Act riots of the 1830s Sir John Musters' castle was set on fire. Sir John and Lady Chaworth were staying at the castle and had to flee from the rioters and hide in the park. Lady Chaworth was able to rescue her jewellery box from the fire, but lost it as she ran into the darkness. The story has it that she caught a chill that night which killed her. The jewels were never found and her restless spirit is said to be seen hopelessly searching for them.

CUCKNEY

The Grey Lady and Dick Turpin

THE village is properly known as Norton Cuckney, but over time it has become separated into two halves. Norton is now a sleepy hamlet but was once the centre of this community. The old coaching route from Mansfield to Worksop ran through the centre of the village and, at one time, the road brought Norton Cuckney enough passing trade to sustain three pubs. With the advent of the motor car and the increased traffic, the Duke of Portland provided land so that the main road could be diverted through Cuckney. The focal point of the village moved as trade now focused on the busier new road, the modern A60. Norton became a quiet backwater as Cuckney grew. However, reminders of Norton's coaching days linger still. On Packhorse Row, on the old blacksmith's shop, you can still see the lintel for the sign for the Packhorse Inn. Local tradition has it that this inn was one of the many hideouts of Dick Turpin (1706 to 1739). In St Mary's church, Cuckney, walks the ghost known as the Grey Lady. Local folklore has it that she is always seen in the first row of pews on the right-hand side. Her identity and her reason for haunting the church have become lost in the mists of time.

EDWINSTOWE

'For Sale – Secondhand car, excellent condition – Haunted'!

FROM a librarian in Edwinstowe comes this story of a haunted car. A young local couple were looking to buy themselves a family car. The husband worked at the near-by pit and his wife had a part-time job in the village. They wanted something affordable and practical, 'a good clean motor'. With these requirements in mind, they toured the local car dealers' forecourts. On a Saturday morning in November they found a vehicle to meet all their needs, a hatchback, in excellent condition, at a very good price. The husband was a little suspicious, the paint was too new, he suspected a re-spray, the mileage was very low for a car of this registration. He spoke to the dealer who informed him that it was entirely genuine, the car had only just arrived and was priced for a quick sale. After a test drive the couple decided to buy it. Terms were agreed and the dealer promised to forward the log book as soon as he received it in the post.

All went well and the car proved an excellent 'runner'. The husband's change of shifts meant that he had the car mostly but, when convenient, his wife would drop him off at the pit and have the car to herself. On a dank morning, before seven, the tired miner drove home. He'd done some overtime and was looking forward to a hot bath and a long sleep. Up ahead a milk float stopped on his side of the road. Checking in the rearview mirror, before pulling out, he saw something large lurch from one side of the car's back seat to the other. Startled, he turn his head to see, illuminated by the yellow neon glow of the street lights, a horribly disfigured corpse, whose dead eyes looked straight at him. He slammed on the brakes, narrowly missing the milk float. Transfixed, he stared at the horribly injured body. In terror he leapt from the car and ran up the road to the milk float. It was some minutes before he could make the startled milkman understand there was a body on the back seat of his car. Cautiously they walked back to the abandoned vehicle, together they gingerly peered through the rear window, there was nothing there. They searched the immediate area – nothing. Sympathetically, the milkman suggested that perhaps the miner had been working too hard and had experienced some sort of hallucination. Calmer now, the miner agreed and continued on his way home, deciding to say nothing to his wife as she might worry.

On the day shift once more, it was his wife's turn to have the car. After a busy morning at work and with the week's shopping to do, she called in at a petrol station to fill up. Whilst paying at the counter her attention was suddenly drawn to her car. 'There's someone stealing my car,' she cried and dashed across the forecourt. Grabbing open the door, she froze in horror as a body, terribly mutilated, fell out onto the tarmac. Screaming, she ran back into the garage shop. The equally terrified assistant calmed her down and rang for the police. Both were too disturbed to approach the car themselves and waited for the arrival of the police. To their relief, they were quick to respond. However, the officers found no trace of a body, no blood, no signs of violence, nothing. The policemen, understandably, insisted on a breath test. This proved negative, and after the careful reassurance of the officers, the lady went home. On collecting her husband from work, she was surprised by his grave and silent attention to her story.

'I didn't want to tell you this,' he said, 'but I saw the same thing but thought I'd imagined it.' Later that same evening a policeman visited the couple. He informed them that the car had been run through the police computer. It had been in a fatal accident. It hadn't been 'written off', as only the rear of the car was damaged in a freak accident with a lorry that left a passenger dead. The next morning an envelope arrived in the post. It was the log book, showing the car had had six previous owners in two years. Immediately they decided to get rid of it. That same morning the husband returned to the car dealer and he was offered two hundred pounds less for the car than he paid for it. He accepted the offer without hesitation, and the dealer asked no questions. Perhaps the car is waiting now on some forecourt – 'For Sale – Excellent Condition – Haunted'. A modern myth or a cautionary tale? Either way, *caveat emptor*, let the buyer beware.

EGMANTON

The Singing Ghost

MR AND MRS Ilett, the same couple who were woken by the ghostly brickworks at Boughton, lived at one time in Egmanton, in a cottage formerly belonging to the Portland estate. They named the cottage 'Tangle Wood'. Late at night the couple often heard the sound of a ghostly child singing in the entrance hall. Mrs Ilett remembers, 'There were a lot of tales told locally about this cottage. It is over three hundred years old. We had quite a few odd things happen. We often used to hear this child singing, if we'd sat up late at night till two or three o'clock. The first couple of times this happened we'd get up and look. It seemed to come from the entrance hall, but there was no way it could. It definitely sounded like a little girl. You couldn't make out what she was singing, but you could tell that she was being accompanied on a harpsichord. It used to last a couple of seconds then go.'

GREAT NORTH ROAD

Highwaymen and Phantom Coaches

THE old Great North Road ran along the eastern edge of the county through the towns of Newark, Tuxford and East Retford. The old road has now been bypassed by the A1, but for centuries it was the main route from London to York and beyond. Many of the coaching inns still survive from those days, like pearls on a string. With a constant ebb and flow of human life, the old Great North Road has ghosts and legends all of its own.

Wealthy travellers on the road proved a magnet for footpads and highwaymen and many were relieved of their valuables with the cry 'Your money or your life!' Dick Turpin, the most famous highwayman of them all, held up many a coach on the Great North Road. The best known Nottinghamshire highwayman was John 'Swift Nick' Nevison (b.1639–d.1685), so called, it is said, by King Charles II himself. Some sources suggest it was Nevison, and not Turpin, who made the famous London to York ride to establish an alibi. Nevison's gang of six outlaws met at the Talbot Inn at Newark and robbed travellers along the Great North Road as far north as York and as far south as Huntingdon. The gang were betrayed in 1676 by one Elizabeth Burton after she was arrested for stealing. Nevison was transported to Tangiers, but returned to England in 1681 and once more took to highway robbery. Although King Charles offered a reward for his recapture, Nevison remained at large for four years. When he was finally apprehended, his trial judge showed no mercy and Nevison was sentenced to hang at York. On the morning of 15th March 1685 Nevison mounted the scaffold. He gave a speech to the huge crowd that had gathered in which he asked for forgiveness for his crimes and warned others not to follow in his path. Having said his piece, 'Swift Nick' was dispatched by the hangman. The body was buried at St Mary's church, York, in an unmarked grave.

Dickens described a coaching mishap on the road just

before Newark in *The Pickwick Papers*. Another tale told in coaching days has been updated and is still around today. Originally it went like this: A coach was travelling along the Great North Road with a young married couple aboard. Midway between towns the coach lost a wheel, and the coachmen decided to walk on to the next stop to summon help. The couple inside the coach were quite happy at first to be left alone. Darkness began to fall and the night grew cold. Impatient at the long delay, and fearing his new wife would get a chill, the husband resolved to walk a little way up the road himself and watch for the coachmen whilst there was still light to see by. The lady sat alone, keeping warm as best she could. After some time she became anxious for her husband's return, but feared the inky darkness outside. She was soon reassured when she heard voices approaching. Her relief turned to alarm when she heard shouts and the sounds of running men. Someone jumped up on the roof of the coach and it began to sway alarmingly, then loud thumps above threatened to bring the roof down upon her. Scrambling to the window, she was dazzled by the light of many lamps and she shaded her eyes with her hand. Then a voice from what seemed a crowd called to her, 'Miss! You must open the door slowly and walk towards the light. On no account look behind you!' Trembling, she open the door and on unsteady legs walked towards the silent lamp-bearers. When almost to them, she turned to look back at the coach. There on the roof, caught in the lamplight, crouched a man. His features were horribly twisted with rage and his eyes were the wild red unseeing eyes of a raving lunatic. As she watched, the snapped chains from the manacles at his wrists began to flay about him, as he banged her husband's severed head on the roof of the coach. In the modern version the coach has become a car that has run out of petrol, but the story remains the same.

In bygone days Nottinghamshire folk using the road would like to get home before dark as they might encounter the 'Owd Lad', the Devil himself in his black coach and four. One old carrier is said have seen it drive past him, 'all on fire like brimstone, pulled by four skeleton horses'. Another legend has it that on moonlit nights a coach and six, driven by a headless coachman, conveying a headless, richly dressed nobleman, is seen rattling down the road at a furious pace. The coach, horses and headless phantoms then vanish as suddenly as they appeared.

HOLME

Nan Scott – the Face at the Window

BY 1666 the Great Plague had reached Nottinghamshire. It had already claimed about a fifth of the population of London, and as it began thinning the population of Newark the villagers of Holme, north of the town, could only look on in horror and pray. One villager, Anne Scott, known as Nan, began to hoard food and drink.

Seeking divine deliverance from the plague, Nan Scott sought sanctuary within the church. Above the south door of St Giles' is a small chamber. Nan bolted herself into this tiny room and became a virtual recluse, while around her the death toll in Holme mounted. With her hoard of food and drink to sustain her Nan watched the world from a window above the porch. At first the church services continued and the sounds drifted up to Nan and comforted her. From her window she saw the funerals increase in frequency from several a week, to one a day, to several a day, until the dignified, orderly burials were replaced with handcarts and mass graves. Whole families, whole streets died together. Activity beyond the window slowed, then stopped. Those who weren't dead had fled. The village became a ghost town. To many at the time the plague seemed like the end of the world, divine retribution on a wicked world. To Nan it must have seemed she was the last person left on the earth.

When life did return to Holme, Nan was found dead. Tradition has it that she stayed in her chamber and either starved to death or died of loneliness. The church became once more the centre of village life. Local people commented, however, that someone was often seen peering out of the porch window down onto the comings and goings below. The general opinion was that it was Nan's ghost, still forlornly gazing out onto a dead world, vainly hoping for the rescue that never came. If you visit the church of St Giles, pause a moment at the porch and look up – a face at the window might be looking back at you.

HUTHWAITE

The Haunted Library

HUTHWAITE, near Sutton-in-Ashfield, is a small township that grew out of the old village of Hucknall Huthwaite. The chief urban amenities came late to Huthwaite, such as the National School built in 1867 under the direction of the Rev Charles Bellairs, Vicar of Sutton. Huthwaite didn't even have its own curate until 1873, when one was provided by the largess of such worthies as the Dowager Countess of Caernarvon, the Hon C.I. Lyttelton and William H. Gladstone MP. The building of the village church was similarly funded. The foundation stone was laid in 1902 by her Grace the Duchess of Portland, accompanied by the Duke, who gave generously towards the building fund. It was opened in 1905 by the Bishop of Southwell. In 1907 the village dropped 'Hucknall' from its name and adopted its current form. The culmination of this period of civic development was the opening of the library on Saturday, 12th April 1913. The building was funded by the Carnegie initiative, which provided the libraries for many towns and cities across the country. It is typical of the design adopted for the Carnegie libraries, but the Huthwaite library has the added appeal of a resident ghost.

The library was built in the park between the junction of Sutton Road and Columbia Street. A pond was drained to provide the site, and it seems this disturbed the ghost that has haunted the library ever since. The pond had been the scene of a tragedy. A woman had drowned herself there. Her body had lain for some time on the pond's muddy bottom before rising to the surface, from where it was recovered and duly buried. The discreet sensibilities of Huthwaite folk have drawn a veil over this sad event and we now do not know the woman's identity or what drove her to take her own life.

However, soon after the opening of the library, her ghost was seen wandering among the bookshelves. Since that time she has been spotted several times, especially when changes are made to the library, such as redecoration. Recently her most vivid appearance has been to a cleaner. 'Mrs H', a long-time resident of Huthwaite, had worked at the library for many years before retiring. She had often felt that unnerving sensation of being watched when she was alone on the premises. Though she was aware of the library's haunted reputation she hadn't given it much thought until she saw the ghost with her own eyes.

One afternoon whilst completing her usual routine Mrs H was startled to see someone standing in the library not far from her. The library was closed, the doors locked, and as far as she was aware she was alone in the building. Thinking to assist the lady, Mrs H approached the figure, and as she did so she noticed the woman's clothes. The dress she wore was grey silk, and unmistakably Victorian or Edwardian, her hair was carefully styled and, although not old, she was mature rather than young. No sooner had Mrs H become aware of these impressions than the figure disappeared. Though this experience left a strong impression on Mrs H she wasn't overly concerned, and continued to work alone on the premises until her retirement.

None of the staff currently at the library have seen the Lady-in-Grey, but she does make her presence felt on occasion. Huthwaite's haunted library is well worth a visit. The library staff report that Huthwaite has two other local ghosts – the figure of an old man walking with a stick on Mill Lane, and a ghost at the Wood End pub.

KIRKBY-IN-ASHFIELD

Ghosts Duel for a Castle

IN November 1989 Mr Ernest Harker, of Matlock Bath, Derbyshire, was walking with his granddaughter Jane in some woods near Kirkby-in-Ashfield, Nottinghamshire. Though it was a cold day the winter sun was shining brightly and there was no wind. Mr Harker describes what happened next:

'We had just walked up the hill when I heard the sounds of a violent fight. It sounded like quite a number of people. At first I thought maybe hunt saboteurs had broken up a hunt, and it had turned ugly. I couldn't think why else people would be fighting in the wood. Men were shouting and I could hear blows being exchanged. I was worried about the girl, but couldn't see where the sound was coming from. Then I distinctly heard someone shouting "He's dead, he's dead!" and the fight got worse. I could hear the sound of people running towards us, then past us. By now my granddaughter was crying so I picked her up and made off quick. I don't know what it was but it was a very unpleasant experience I can tell you.'

It would seem that somehow Ernest Harker and his granddaughter had heard the sounds of the battle for Kirkby Castle that had occurred 430 years before.

Sir Charles Cavendish and Sir John Stanhope were rivals. At any and every opportunity they sought to outshine each other, at the hunt, in the county and at the court of Queen Elizabeth I. Both enjoyed high living and they were both in debt. Sir John sought to improve his lot by applying to the Crown for the rights to some land that had once been monastic property. He paid out heavy bribes to court officials to see he got it. Meanwhile, Sir Charles looked for a wealthy heiress.

In the midst of his financial difficulties Sir John fell foul of the law. It seems that a beggar had been making a nuisance of himself on Sir John's estate and despite a sound thrashing still lingered about the place. Sir John took matters into his own hands and had the beggar hanged from a tree. However, when the Justices came to hear of this *Sir John* was summoned for usurping the Queen's pre-rogative, and was tried by his peers in the House of Lords, at great expense to himself. He was found guilty and heav-ily fined, returning home much the poorer and with greater need than ever for the rents of the disputed lands. He paid out further gratuities to oil the machinery of gov-ernment and waited. His patience was not rewarded; not only was his claim unsuccessful, but the lands went to his rival Sir Charles Cavendish, who had meanwhile found his rich heiress, Ruth Sachaverill, and married her. Sir John had, up to this point, always retained a dignified civility in his dealings with his rival. However, this was replaced by utter contempt when he learned that Sir Charles had won, not because of the beggar's death, but simply because he had paid greater bribes to the court officials. One thought alone possessed Sir John, revenge. He challenged Sir Charles to a duel, but Sir Charles simply refused to meet him.

Sir Charles, in newly found married bliss, was taken up with plans for a new, grand house. He planned to build it on the very land he had won from his rival and to call it Kirkby Castle. Omens and portents were still given much credence in Elizabethan England and Sir Charles consulted a local soothsayer, an aged crone who lived as a hermit in the woods of Hagnook, about the building of Kirkby Castle. The wise-woman said that the site for the house was a most auspicious one. However, she added that noth-ing but bad luck would fall on the house and its owners if any blood were spilt there during its construction. In June 1559 Sir Charles ordered work to start on Kirkby Castle. This proved the final insult for Sir John and he marched to the site with a body of armed men. Work was well under way, the foundations having been laid. Scattering work-men, Sir John came face to face with Sir Charles, who was supervising the work.

With rapiers drawn and ringed by their servants, the two nobles fought furiously for over an hour. Gradually Sir John began to tire and Sir Charles gained the upper hand. At that moment one of Sir John's men stuck out a foot and caused Sir Charles to fall. The fight now became general between the two parties. Sir Charles' servants, though out-numbered, managed to drive off Sir John and his men, with the loss of four killed. Both Sir Charles and Sir John were seriously injured, but survived. Their rivalry had burnt itself out and they never fought again. Work on the house stopped and it was not resumed. According to legend, Sir Charles was fearful of the prophecy of the crone of Hagnook. The foundations of Kirkby Castle can still be seen in the woods to this day.

KIRTON

The Jolly Farmer at the Fox and Hounds

THE Fox and Hounds at Kirton has been haunted for years by a ghost known to the regulars as Fred. According to local people, a ghost with the appearance of a 'jolly farmer' was often seen wandering about the pub during the 1970s. In the autumn of 1994 a hedge was dug up and a trench laid in a field at the back of the pub. This activity apparently disturbed the ghost. In a newspaper article of 2nd November 1994 the landlord, Mr Doug Glentworth, told the reporter: 'A neighbour went to put a blanket over one of her horses late one foggy night last week (the end of October) and was alarmed to see that the animals were in a highly agitated state. She went for a closer look and was startled to hear what sounded like voices coming from the trench.'

Mr Glentworth then did some research of his own. The Fox and Hounds is the second pub in the village to bear the name. The present building dates from 1913 and was built adjacent to the site of the old Fox and Hounds after it was demolished. From the old records Mr Glentworth deduced that the trench had been dug right through the site of the old pub. 'Our excavation work must have disturbed some spirits which rest there.' Could this be the case? Might the trench work have disturbed the jolly farmer or are there now other restless spirits at the Fox and Hounds? Mr Glentworth concluded: 'We haven't seen him ourselves but objects have been moved around while nobody was in the room and we've heard some mysterious noises in the night. But so far nothing sinister has happened and my wife and my daughter are happy to stay – and it doesn't worry the customers so why should it worry me?'

LAXTON

The Boggan and Peggy Whooper

'And Brokilow Bridge where as boys we caught frogs.
They say this was haunted, but what was feared most,
Was "Bolembeck Lane" with a real active ghost.
Peggy Whooper her name, no one knows how she died,
But most people think murder, and some suicide.'

(From *My Lifetime of Memories of Laxton* by Frank Moody)

LAXTON is the last village in England where the medieval open-field system still survives. Visitors interested in farming come here from all over the world. Each autumn the Court Baron convenes at the Dovecote Inn to allocate the land to the tenants, who farm it in long, narrow strips, using a crop rotation system. Born and bred in Laxton, Mr Reg Rose has had a life-long interest in farming and the countryside, and he is now the founder and curator of the Laxton Heritage Museum at Lilac Farm. As a boy Reg would talk for hours with the old folk of the village, learning all he could. 'I've memories of people who were born in the 1850s, and their experiences of over 100 years ago. It was from these old characters I heard about the local ghosts and legends.

34

'People used to go miles out of their way not to meet the ghost of Peggy Whooper. She was a farm girl who was murdered on Bolembeck Lane. When you go out of Laxton go along up to the crossroads by Kneesall Woods. As you stand at the crossroads, on your left is Bolembeck Lane, the way to Ossington, on your right is the way to Kneesall. There is a hollow in the road here with a bridge over a stream running from Laxton Lodge. This is where Peggy Whooper was murdered and this is where she haunts. The bridge became known as Peggy Whooper's bridge. This has always been a place to be wary of. It was said horses would shy here for no reason, throwing their rider if they weren't careful.

'I also heard my father tell of another spot where horses would shy. Father used to talk about the Boggan, said to appear on the stretch of road between Parson's Hill and Brokilow Bridge. As a young boy he used to get work on several different farms when he could. He'd go on horse-back along Brokilow Bridge and he had horses shy there. He used to say the horses had sensed the Brokilow Boggan when he couldn't see it. When I talked to father about it he described it as a big animal, a wolf-type hound. The legend was told to me not only by my father, but by my wife's grandfather. People who lived up there often spoke of the Brokilow Boggan. There were various sightings of this thing. The women were especially afraid of meeting the Boggan on the road at night. The Boggan wasn't all bad though. The servant girls and farm hands used to collect on Cross Hill to come from a dance in Laxton. There was a dance floor at the Dovecote Inn and one at Post Office Farm. After a dance you could always suggest to a girl that, "You'd better let me walk you home because of the Boggan!" '

The English Dialect Dictionary of 1898 throws more light on the Brokilow Boggan. A boggan, or boggin, was a hob-goblin or terrible apparition with the same derivation as boggart or boggard, which appears in much of the folklore of northern England. 'Nearly every old house had its bog-gart which played ill-natured tricks on the inhabitants. Singly or in packs they haunted streets and roads, and the arch-boggarts held revel at every 'three-road-end.'

(Waugh, *Come Whoam* 1856). According to *The English Dialect Dictionary*, horses were described as 'boggardly' if timid or skittish. There is no reference to the boggan being a ghost dog, so this may be a use of the word particular to the Laxton area.

Reg knows of other ghosts in the village: 'There has often been talk of Lilac Farm being haunted. We've never seen anything but we do get this weird smell. It's always the same smell. I've searched for the source many times. It's obnoxious. It comes in one of the first floor rooms and moves towards the bathroom, in what was the old servants' quarters. One second it's in one place, the next it's gone and then comes somewhere else. I knew the lady who lived here before us and I know she was frightened to be alone in here and I never could get her to say why.

'In a house now called Dijon House live Les and Joan Fretwell. It used to be an old pub owned by Hewitt's brewery of Sheffield. Long after it was a pub the Bartel family lived there. Jack Bartel was about my age and a great boyhood friend. Jack and his brother Norman would often say they saw this figure standing at the end of their bed. Norman described it to me as a Cromwellian soldier in full uniform. Many people who have lived at that house have seen this ghost. Les Fretwell has told me that he has also seen this figure, and it definitely looked like a Civil War soldier. If two people tell you something 60 years apart it makes you think, doesn't it?'

The 12th-century church of St Michael was somewhat unsympathetically restored in 1860. However, this has not rid it of its ghost. Reg has had some knowledge of this wraith: 'As a boy I never liked to walk through the churchyard. Years later I converted the church heating system from coke to diesel. I had to go to the church in the middle of the night to check that the diesel burner had fired up all right. Old Saddington, the local joiner, wheelwright and undertaker, was the churchwarden. He used to tell me that he'd heard footsteps and other odd noises in the church when there was no one about. He used to pull my leg about it. Sitting in the boiler hole, I did feel a little apprehensive. I heard all sorts of bumps and bangs but paid no attention to them. However, we did have a parson here who was scared stiff of going in the church at night. He'd been in the vestry in the north chancel behind the organ, when he felt there was something behind him. He turned round and saw a figure standing there, what it was he would never say. Churches are eerie places at night.'

MANSFIELD

The Bessie Sheppard Stone

IN 1817 Bessie Sheppard was murdered on the road between Mansfield and Ravenshead. Bessie left home on the morning of 7th July to walk to Mansfield in search of work as a domestic servant. She wore her new shoes for the occasion and carried a brightly coloured cotton umbrella. She was seen leaving Mansfield at 6 o'clock on her return home. She never arrived. Her body was found early the next morning in a ditch by the roadside, about 50 yards south of the third milestone. Her skull was horribly smashed in, and a large bloodied hedgestake lay near the body. All that same day Charles Rotherham of Sheffield had been drinking. The one-time scissor grinder's apprentice and ex-soldier was seen at the Hut Tavern, Newstead, soon after the murder took place. It seems that Bessie simply happened be in the wrong place at the wrong time. Rotherham beat her to death after she passed him on the road. He searched the body for money, but had found none and stole the only items of value on her person, her shoes and her umbrella. That night at the Three Crowns Inn in Redhill he attempted to sell the pitiful booty. There were no buyers and he left the shoes in his room at the inn. The umbrella was eventually sold in the village of Bunny, on the other side of Nottingham. After his arrest at Loughborough, Rotherham made a full confession. He could give no reason for the murder but want of money. He said he hit Bessie on the head and just kept hitting her until she was dead. On 25th July 1817 Charles Rotherham was hanged for his crime at Gallows Hill in Nottingham.

As an expression of the public's sympathy Mr Anthony Bukles and some other Mansfield businessmen paid for a permanent memorial of the tragedy. At the spot where the body was found a stone was set up with the following inscription: 'This stone was erected in the memory of Elizabeth Sheppard, of Papplewick, who was murdered by Charles Rotherham, near this place, on the 7th of July 1817, aged 17 years.' The inscription has all but weathered away over the years. When the A60 was widened the stone was moved and re-erected on the new verge. Local folklore has it that Bessie's ghost has been disturbed as a result. Since that time local newspapers have periodically reported sightings of a ghost on the A60. Motorists have seen the spectral form of a young woman at the roadside, some having to swerve to avoid her, only to see her vanish.

A Gallery of Ghosts

MANSFIELD is a historic market town, with a theatre, an art gallery, cinemas and an indoor shopping centre. The old market square at the heart of the town was the cattle market until 1877. In the town centre are many fine old pubs and inns, some of which are haunted.

The New Inn, at the top of Westgate, is said to be the second oldest pub in town, second only to Ye Olde Ramme. The frontage of the building is of the blonde-coloured Mansfield stone which was highly sought after in prestigious building projects from stately homes to churches. Indeed, the front of the pub is the oldest part of the building, the rear being extended over the years to provide a greater capacity for business. It is in the front part of the pub that the ghost has been heard, rather than seen. The landlord and his wife, Martin and Jackie Buxton, told me about their experiences. Said Mr Buxton: 'The first time I heard it was late one night. We had not been here all that long. We were just clearing up and we could hear these noises of someone walking around upstairs. I didn't think much of it. I thought my daughter had come back from the night club and the sounds were her. The sounds continued for a bit and then my daughter arrived home – she came into the pub to see us. I asked her if she'd been upstairs and she said she hadn't, she'd only just got in. The next time we were all downstairs and we heard the same thing again, footsteps walking around upstairs. I thought we might have a burglar; but there was nothing upstairs at all. I sent the dog up before me and I remember he wasn't too keen. Sometime after that we were having a late night drink in the bar with some friends. My daughter was upstairs in her room. There was the most almighty crash, like the roof, or the chimney, had fallen in. Several of us rushed upstairs, we met my daughter coming out of her room looking shaken. We could find no cause whatsoever for the sound. It was really very frightening. We have heard the footsteps many times since but not the terrible crashing noise.'

No explanation for the stomping ghost or the crashing sound has been found. No accounts of a death resulting from a roof, or chimney, collapsing at the New Inn have been found either. However, at one time the inn was connected to a terrace of buildings that linked it to Cromwell House, which is also said to be haunted. There are two ghosts here, one in the attic, the other on the stairs. The building is named after Dr Samuel Cromwell, who lived in it from 1680 to about 1720. Cromwell House was once a school; in 1788 the Rev Samuel Catlow, a Nonconformist minister, opened a 'literary and commercial seminary' here. The seminary was so successful that it was extended into the adjoining building in 1800. This building connected Cromwell House to the New Inn, and at the time of demolition in the late 1960s it was Glenie's Dental Surgery. The ghost in the attic is said to be that of a schoolboy who, through homesickness and a poor diet, pined away and died. The other ghost is said to be that of a maid, whose misty shape is seen busily cleaning the stairs. Mr David Wilson, an accountant, has worked in the building for over 30 years and told me he had never seen or heard of any ghosts there, nor had his long-serving predecessor ever mentioned it. However, one of the secretaries did confess to feeling not particularly comfortable when retrieving documents from the attic storeroom. She said she felt as though she was being watched and she was always pleased to leave the attic as quickly as possible.

On the far side of the market place, in Church Street, stands the White Hart Inn. A Tudor building that has undergone many alterations over the years, the inn was a thriving commercial hotel in the 19th century. During the reign of Henry VII this was the residence of Mansfield's wealthiest couple, Robert and Cecily Flogan. Robert died without issue, leaving Cecily, later Dame Flogan, a very rich but lonely widow. She devoted herself to all manner of charitable works, and even made sure that after her death her estate would continue to provide for charity. This included the provision of a 'stout bull and a boar for free use in the parish', presumably for breeding purposes. Her death was sudden and tragic. She was killed in an accident in the stables behind the inn, involving a horse and carriage. It is this traumatic end, to a good and useful life, that, some say, has bound Dame Flogan's spirit to the White Hart Inn. Her shade is seen walking about the building, especially on the stairs and landing leading into the bar. Several employees have seen her there. She also makes her presence felt in the cellar. Bar staff going down there have found themselves inexplicably locked in. One barmaid refused to go down into the cellar ever again after just such an experience. Rob, the manager, whilst having never seen the ghost himself, does feel a presence in the building. The ghost has also been seen outside in Dame Flogan Street and in White Hart Street. It was here that her crushed and bloodied body was dragged after the accident that killed her.

Further along Church Street stands what is reputedly the oldest pub in Mansfield, Ye Olde Ramme. Said to have been built before the church to provide lodgings and beer for the workmen, Ye Olde Ramme is connected to St Peter's by a tunnel. The pub is reported to be haunted by the ghost of a monk. There is a mention of 'Ye Tenne Chantry priests land' on Church Street, in a charter of 1558. Why the monk haunts the pub is unknown, but he has been seen many times. The Ramme itself is well worth a visit, for the ghost, for the excellent beer, and its convivial clientele. In conversation with three regulars at the Ramme, the 'two Lens' and 'Big Arthur', I learnt that the monk is often seen before some disaster or calamity, such as a fire or the price of beer going up! The 'two Lens' remembered several Mansfield characters of the past. These included 'Brown Bomber'- who fished out the bodies of suicides from the reservoir on behalf of the police for the odd shilling – and 'Nuts-a-penny', who sold gingernuts around the town's pubs. They told me of other haunted pubs in the town, namely the Wheatsheaf, the King's Head, and the Plough Inn on Nottingham Road. Arthur recalls the tale of the ghost at the Ransom Hospital. It is the ghost of a nurse who jumped from the roof of the building after she was spurned by a doctor. Her shade, in a Victorian nurse's uniform, is seen in the hospital and flitting amidst the trees of the nearby wood.

The Bridge Tavern is the lowest point below sea level in the town and is prone to flooding. The pub itself has expanded over the years into several adjacent buildings, one of which was, at one time, the town morgue. This is now the main seating area of the pub. The landlord told me that the river flows beneath the building. It is said that in the past a trapdoor in the floor was used to drop the occasional corpse straight into the waters below. Denied proper burial, maybe some unquiet spirits linger here still. The eerie feeling of being watched has been experienced both by staff and customers at this end of the pub. Furniture has been rearranged by unseen hands at night and odd bumps and bangs have disturbed after-hours drinkers.

The pub was the scene of a tragedy. On the night of Saturday, 15th November 1959 a fight broke out in the bar and the landlord, Mr Charlie Strout, intervened. Some time after the fight Charlie collapsed and died. It was first rumoured that he had received a stab wound, but later tests showed he suffered a fatal heart attack. Charlie Strout was an enormously popular host and his death at 48 came as a great shock to his friends, family and customers alike; he is still well remembered in the town. Whether the odd occurrences at the pub are due to Charlie making his presence felt, or the belated protests of those who left the premises via the trapdoor, remains unknown.

Near Mansfield's fire station is a row of semi-detached Victorian houses. These 'villas' are spacious, solidly built and make ideal family homes. Mark (his surname is omitted to protect his privacy), with a young and growing family, bought one of them. The house needed some work, but Mark was quite handy with DIY and he began a series of alterations. In an interview, Mark told me the story: 'Every time I did something to the house odd things happened. If I knocked a wall out or did a door, we'd get these problems. I had been knocking the kitchen about, the kitchen was about eight foot square. I knocked a pantry and a coalhouse through and made one big room. One night we were lying in bed and we could hear someone coming upstairs. It sounded as if it was someone out of breath and they were coming up one step at a time; it was as if they were stopping for a break. Every stair that creaked when we used the stairs was creaking now as this person made their way up. This went on for between ten minutes and a quarter of an hour. As it came to the bedroom door, I tried to get the wife to get up and have a look, but she wouldn't. It came right up to the door and stopped. I was convinced there was someone in the house. I dived out of bed, swung the door open and just ran at them. There was no one there, so I ran through every room in the house as fast as I could. I was thinking they had jumped out through the windows, but everything was as it was when we went to bed. This was the worst occasion. There was no central heating in then, no gas pipes, it wasn't an air lock causing a knocking sound. When I bought the house I had to replace every bit of pipework, all the way from the stop-tap in the ground, the tanks and everything. Another time we were sitting downstairs, on a summer's evening about 7 pm, when we heard the sound of breaking glass, just like someone throwing a brick through a window. I went upstairs into our bedroom and the mirror from the dressing table was lying on the floor. All the ornaments and the perfumes were strewn all over the bedroom, but nothing was broken. The things were spread in about a five foot radius, on the bed as well as the floor. We just couldn't explain it at all. After this I tried to find out about the history of the house. An elderly neighbour told me that a preacher or pastor lived here at one time. Since I've finished the major jobs, we've had nothing since. A couple of times the pots on the draining-board rattle; that stops when you go into the kitchen. There are no railways nearby to cause vibrations, so I just don't know.'

This is a typical 'heard and not seen' domestic haunting. All old houses have creaks and noises, but the experiences of Mark and his family would suggest that the alterations to the house did cause some unusual reactions. Whether this is the 'memory' of the house itself, replaying the sounds of the past, or an actual spirit of a long dead resident making its presence felt is a matter for conjecture.

Fear and Loathing on Bottle Lane

ON the corner of Bottle Lane and Nottingham Road once stood an old cottage. A single act of unkindness committed here resulted in one man's death and possibly the suicide of another, which left the premises haunted. The cottage was once an inn called 'Ye Leather Bottell' and for centuries this was the last pub in Mansfield before reaching the Hutt at Newstead. The inn was lived in by several generations of the Martyn family. It was said that outside the hostelry was a large stone with an inscription that read, 'John Martyn's stone I am, Show ye great road to Nottyngham. 1621.' The long history of Ye Leather Bottell ended following the tragic events one stormy night at the end of the 18th century.

A postman called Baggaley left Nottingham on foot, bearing the Mansfield post. A blizzard blew in and great snowdrifts threatened to smother the road. Baggaley tramped on through Sherwood Forest until he reached the Hutt at Newstead. Almost frozen, he took shelter here and rested a while, before resuming his journey. The snow grew worse. Baggaley struggled on until he reached Ye Leather Bottell. Banging on the door, he asked for food and shelter in the king's name, but contrary to all ancient customs of hospitality he was refused. Baggaley was forced to try and reach Mansfield town itself. Exhaustion and the cold overcame him and he died in the snow near the Water

Meadows. His frozen body was found soon after with the mail bags still clasped in his dead hands. The local justices, on hearing how Baggaley had been left to his fate, held a special sitting and closed down Ye Leather Bottell for ever. The building and land passed to the Townsend family and through them to the Miss Dickons, of Mansfield. It is said that in the 19th century the stone with John Martyn's inscription on was found in the cellar.

In about 1932 a little girl and her family moved into what had been Ye Leather Bottell. Mrs Brooke, as she is now, was about six years old and clearly remembers the events that followed: 'I had two younger sisters, one about 15 months old and the other barely a toddler. It was a large old house on Bottle Lane, Mansfield. My father rented it cheap as it had been empty a long time. It was a damp and nasty old place, with a smell of stale beer. My mother spent hours cleaning it up to make it fit to live in. There was gas but no electricity. There was a single large room downstairs, with the cellar beneath, a big back kitchen and one big bedroom upstairs we all shared.'

'Years later Mother told me what had happened to her in that room. She had insisted on sleeping on the outside of the bed, so as to be able to get to the baby if it woke in the night. The baby had been restless since we arrived. One night as she lay in bed she looked across the room to where we children slept and saw this figure of a man standing over the cot. She knew it was a ghost, and was frightened and woke my father. He wasn't happy to be woken and even less so when she asked to swop sides of the bed. He wouldn't get up, so she pulled the bedclothes over her head and lay there all night. The following night the baby woke again. As she rolled over to see to the child she saw this face lying on the pillow next to her. Although terrified, she clearly saw the man; he had a ginger moustache, a balding head, and a light coloured apron tied at the front. She felt icy cold and couldn't breathe. When she got her breath again, she woke Father, who still wouldn't get up. Next morning she told him exactly what she'd seen. Father didn't say a word. He'd known the house was haunted from the outset, someone had told him on the dole queue that the place had been left empty so long because of the ghost. Father had heard that a man had hanged himself in the cellar, from a hook in the ceiling. That wasn't all. Two young cousins, Ted and Eric, helped my father to move. They stayed over that night, sleeping downstairs on the sofa in front of the fire. Next day Father came downstairs to find them both ready to leave, they wouldn't even stay for breakfast. They had passed a disturbed night. Ted had been woken by a figure peeping over the top of the sofa at them. He had kicked his brother to wake him and he saw the same thing, in the flickering firelight. They got up and turned the gas light on. There was no one else in the room but them. They sat up all night with the gas full on, too frightened to go back to sleep. Ted and Eric told my father that they wouldn't stop another night if he paid them!

'We had been there about a fortnight. Mother and Father agreed to move and went out to look at another place to live. They didn't go far, just over the road to look at some rooms for let. I was left sitting by the fire threading beads on a string whilst my sisters slept upstairs. All of a sudden I heard this awful scream from the children upstairs. I looked to the stairfoot-door and heard someone come down the stairs. I knew it wasn't my baby sisters and I just froze. Then the latch on the door lifted and it swung open. It came out of the dark like a shadow, just an outline of a man. I could see him clearly, the moustache, the balding head, and these horrible eyes. It floated sideways, then drifted backwards, still facing me, into the cellar. When my voice came back to me I let out one terrible scream. I ran out into the yard but couldn't open the gates. I screamed and screamed. Before I knew it Mother and Father were back. I couldn't speak. A policeman came and I was in such a state the doctor was sent for. He gave me something to make me sleep and I was sent to my grandma's house to recover. Mother told me it was just a dream, she said nothing to me then about what she'd seen or what happened to Ted and Eric.

'Years later, when I was married with children and living in Yorkshire, my mother sent me a newspaper cutting about the demolition of that old house. It seems that the workers pulling it down had all sort of problems, tools mysteriously going missing, strange noises and the like. They were only too happy to finish the job. This confirms all that had happened to us all those years ago.'

Was the haunting experienced by Mrs Brooke and her family in any way connected to the death of Baggaley the postman? Was it the landlord of Ye Leather Bottell that hanged himself in the cellar after he lost his licence and in remorse for leaving the postman to his fate? The description given by Mrs Brooke certainly fits that of a landlord in an apron. With the house now demolished, we can only wonder.

MANSFIELD WOODHOUSE

Tunnels under Mansfield Woodhouse

THE Woodhouse tunnels are said to connect the Manor to the church, with the exit emerging within the church itself. Another is said to run from the Manor House to the High Street, emerging beneath Wolfhunt House, an ancient building, now a wool shop. Further up the street, Cross Hill Cottage is said to have a priest hole dating back to the Civil War – one of the rooms is smaller inside than it appears to be from the outside and is thought to have a false wall concealing the hiding place. If the cottage was a Royalist 'safe-house' it could well be connected to the tunnel network. Behind the building society premises on the High Street is a large 17th-century house that conceals another entrance to the tunnel complex. Some of the Woodhouse tunnels are for sewage and drainage but the careful construction of the others suggests their covert purposes. It is possible that the staunch Royalist Sir John Digby, who lived in the Manor House built by his grandfather in the late 16th century, planned to mount a stern defence of the house and that this resistance would be supplied via the tunnels.

Haunted Wd'hus Pubs

ON High Street in Mansfield Woodhouse is the Angel, said to be the oldest pub in the village. The Angel is haunted by three ghosts, those of an old woman and a child upstairs and the shade of a man sitting downstairs in the pub. I spoke to the landlord and his wife and they said that they had heard the stories about the pub being haunted. Several residents of the pub have, down the years, reported seeing an apparition of a lady in the private apartments upstairs. This figure has most usually been spotted at the top of the stairs.

Just off the main bar area is a panelled room with a 'cold spot', where an unnatural chill can make one feel most uncomfortable. This part of the pub was originally a wholly separate building. Samantha, one of the bar staff, has seen the ghost of an old man sitting in this room. Samantha confesses an interest in spiritualism and believes she is sensitive to psychic forces. She told me of her experiences whilst working in the pub: 'When I first came here I noticed it was always cold in that room. The woman who appears upstairs is supposed to be seen straight above this room. The thing I've seen is in the far end of the room; in the right-hand corner.'

At this point we walked into the 'wooden room', which was entirely empty. The room was distinctly colder than the rest of the pub, and had a quite separate feel from the lively atmosphere near the bar. We resumed our conversation, but the tape recording made at the time reveals we were now, quite unconsciously, almost whispering. Sam continued to tell me about the room: 'We use this room as the restaurant. Right now I've got "butterflies". Every time I come in here I get them. Well, one night I was in this room and got this feeling, just as I moved into the corner to clear the glasses. I saw a shadow in the corner here, just like there was someone sitting behind me. I turned and there was no one there. I turned away. Then an actual movement caught my eye. I looked and an old man was sitting there, just like a shadow but with no one there to make it. I can sense it now as we talk. It has happened since, I've seen him again out of the corner of my eye.'

By now there was a definite chill in the air, and though it

was middle of the day, in a room just off a busy public bar, there was a certain atmosphere building up in the room. We were both starting to feel decidedly uncomfortable. Sam continued her story: 'When I first came here I did a reading and soon became aware of a presence, one that you definitely did not want to approach further. I've gone all cold now telling you. I did the reading in this corner, where I saw the apparition. As I did this reading I could feel this presence getting stronger. It is definitely that of a man, an elderly man. The person I was doing the reading for, she could feel it too. I've been aware of his presence here ever since. I didn't like clearing up there and I'd say to the previous manager, "Geoff, you can do the wooden room" and he'd laugh. It seems he and his wife had the same experience in here, long before I even suggested it, and knew why I didn't like the room. In here you get two or three people sitting in groups, and nobody ever sits in that corner at all.' Since I interviewed Sam the landlord has moved the pool table into this little-used room.

Further along High Street is the Portland Arms. At the very apex of its roof is a terracotta dragon very similar to those on the roof of the stable block at Rufford Abbey. This heraldic beast is said to ward off evil. It seems to be doing its job, for though the inn is haunted the ghost is an entirely benign spirit. The Portland Arms was once a busy commercial hotel and, like so many hotels in the past, it had a doorman to welcome guests into the premises. The building ceased to function as a hotel some time after the Second World War. However, George the doorman remains on duty even though he has been dead for many years.

It seems that George served as general odd-job man about the place, filling in his time working in the cellar, serving behind the bar and, of course, carrying the luggage of the hotel guests up to their rooms. Standing outside the Portland, George would watch the road for an approaching charabanc or more rarely in those days a private car, bringing new arrivals to the hotel. Exposed to the elements, George would get cold on such occasions and would come into the hotel to warm himself by the fire. His ghostly figure has been seen many times, especially on Friday nights, around 9.20 pm. The lounge was the old foyer for the hotel. It has a stage at one end for the regular live music nights held at the Portland. It would seem, however, that George isn't fond of modern music. Several band members reported to Tom, the barman in 1994, that things, such as guitar leads, plectrums or drum sticks, had gone astray; some to be found later in peculiar places, while other items were never seen again. George's other haunt is the cellar. Tom believes that it was here that George died. It seems he collapsed at the head of the stairs after the exertion of shifting heavy barrels. Tom told me how one morning, after a music night, he came downstairs to find all the electric beer pumps and all the lights in the pub switched on. Tom was sure he had followed his regular routine the night before and switched everything off and he can't account for what happened. Could it have been George, saving Tom the job? Tom, who has since the left the pub, suggested that casual customers could see George, a wholly benign presence, standing by the fireplace and be none the wiser that they were looking on the ghostly doorman of the Portland Arms.

This inn occupies a corner block with another pub, the Parliament Oak, on the junction of High Street with Church Street. Some years back, the landlord of the Parliament Oak was awoken from his bed by the police. On a routine patrol they had found the pub doors were open and all the lights ablaze, despite it being the early hours of the morning. No one was inside and nothing untoward had happened. The landlord was completely mystified and insisted that he had shut shop as usual the night before. The pub is divided into two cosy rooms, the main bar and a snug lounge. It is in the lounge that a presence has been felt by both staff and customers, an unnerving feeling of being watched, especially in the far corner of the room. The rear wall of the lounge adjoins the 'gents', and it was here that one customer had experience enough to put him off drink for good. One Saturday evening, Charlie, alone in the gents, looked up to see a little old lady walk through the wall he was facing, go straight past him and out through the other wall. This encounter so perturbed him that he now never uses those toilets at all. Further down Church Street from the Parliament Oak is the public library. At the back of the library is a small, enclosed garden where a ghostly figure of a little old lady has been seen. Is this the same ghost that walks through the walls of the Parliament Oak? Her identity and the reason for her haunting remains unknown, but could she be walking along a path on which the pub and library now stand?

A Ghost in the Machine

THE old stocking factory on Grove Street, Mansfield Woodhouse, formerly known as Warner's factory, is now called the Anne Frank Building. It is well known locally as a haunted place. Over the years many workers in the factory have experienced uncanny happenings there. Some time ago one of the employees, Mrs Dawson of Mansfield Woodhouse, went into the factory on a Saturday morning. The factory floor was empty and she was alone. All of a sudden the weaving machines started up. The supervisor heard this from the office and came out. Mrs Dawson explained that the machines had started up on their own and the supervisor switched them off. After a few minutes they started up again. There was no one else on the factory floor and no one had switched them on. Both the supervisor and Mrs Dawson were mystified as to the cause. An electrician was sent for and after checking the machines found that there was no electrical fault to account for the machines switching themselves on. Later that same day Mrs Dawson heard the door to the shop floor open and sounds of someone approaching. When she looked up to greet them there was no one there. The precise cause of the haunting remains unknown, but a fatal factory accident in the last century might have something to do with it.

The Ghost with Flaming Red Hair

THE Manor House, sometimes called 'Woodhouse Castle', looks as a haunted house should. The original house has, however, all but disappeared beneath grandiose castellations added to the roof by Captain Need RN, who lived here with his family during the latter part of the 19th century. After many changes of use the house was converted into flats. For many years there has been a local tradition that the Manor was haunted.

Mr Roy Waggott, Secretary of the Old Woodhouse Society, regularly gives illustrated talks on local history and folklore. The following account of the Manor House ghost was given to him by Betty Cartwright-Taylor, whose family lived at the Manor after the Needs left: 'This happened when Betty was about 17 (circa 1929). Her bedroom was on the first floor of the wing close to the church; as you face the Manor it's the window on your left-hand side, near to the balcony above the main entrance. She told me that one morning she woke to find her sister, who shared the room with her, had already got up, dressed and gone downstairs. It was fully daylight and she lay in bed awhile. Suddenly there was a lady with long flaming red hair standing at the side of her bed looking at her. She asked her what she wanted and the lady disappeared. Betty never mentioned this to her family – she was sure that they would have ridiculed her, "Betty's seeing ghosts now", that sort of thing.

'Several years later the Need sisters, who had lived at the Manor until 1911, were visiting Mrs Cartwright-Taylor. They were taking tea in the garden and the conversation came around to ghosts and whether the Manor was haunted. One of the Need sisters exclaimed, "Oh yes, there is a ghost of a lady with flaming red hair that has been seen on several occasions." Betty then said to her mother, "I've seen that lady, Mother, but I didn't say anything because you wouldn't have believed me."

'Betty then told me that on another occasion several years later the butler for their cousins, Mr Ellis of Debdale Hall, was looking after things at the Manor whilst the family all went to church. When the family returned they found the butler greatly agitated. He had been laying out a buffet in the dining room. While he was there a lady appeared, walked through the dining room and out into the hall. He had followed her but she had disappeared. He searched the whole house but couldn't find her. He described her as a lady with flaming red hair.'

Mischievous Spirits

A curious incident happened to Mr Waggott and some members of the Old Woodhouse Society whilst they were visiting an old house scheduled for demolition. Bush House had been the residence of the Tebbit family who had been the surveyors to the Duke of Portland. The last resident of Bush House was a Mr Gregory. Before the building was knocked down to make way for the new Coop superstore the Old Woodhouse Society members visited it to take photographs, measure the rooms and generally record as much about it as possible for posterity. Mr Waggott takes up the story: 'It was summer. One Saturday afternoon at about 1 pm myself, Jim Morris, Keith Page from the Angel Inn and Con Seger, she was a no-nonsense person with a degree in mathematics, arrived at Bush House. We went into the entrance hall which had a flight of stairs leading to the first floor. At the top of these stairs was a landing. The stairs went up again to the right, to an upper landing. I noticed there was a bottle standing upright on the top step of the first landing. I picked it up. It was an old one, with thick green glass, quite empty with no stopper on it. I put it back on the top step. The three men went into a bedroom on the first landing and Con went halfway up the second staircase and stopped for a look around. We were talking when Con said she was being pelted with bobbins of cotton. "They're coming from above." We didn't take much notice. Then again Con said she was being pelted with bobbins. Then there was a crash and Con said, "They've broken this bottle now!"

'We went to look. When we got to it only the base of the bottle, with jagged edges, remained. It was still where I had placed it, but the rest of the bottle had disintegrated. We three men ran outside, I ran towards Welbeck Road, and Keith and Jim ran down onto the High Street, there was no one about. So we thought it must have been someone in the house, we looked all over it but there was no one there. We noticed that there was a bit of furniture left in one room and a box with bobbins and sewing bits and pieces in. This must have been where those thrown at Con had come from.

'Later on, Con had been looking up at the house from outside and wanted to know if a certain window was in the oldest part of the house. I said I'd go back in and look. I passed the bottle on the stairs and noticed the way it had shattered. The whole area was strewn with pieces about an inch across, all over the stairs and the entrance hall, but the base of the bottle hadn't moved. Later I was puzzling over this and I rang Keith Page. He agreed with me that it was all very strange. Later when we looked at the photographic slide that had been taken of the staircase we could see that the bottle, which is in the photograph, hadn't been broken in a normal way. No one could have broken it, or thrown a stone at it, and left the base undisturbed. Since then we have often wondered if we had been in the presence of a poltergeist.'

The White Lady of Mansfield Woodhouse

BLUE Ladies, Grey Ladies, White Ladies and even Green Ladies are a common feature of ghost lore. It has been suggested that these spirits of various colours are echoes of the pre-Christian deities that populated every grove, stream and hill of ancient Britain. The White Lady of Mansfield Woodhouse is a typical example of this type of ghost and seems to haunt several localities.

The ruins of Park Hall brood on the edge of a dank wood. The hall lay empty for many years before being gutted by fire some time after the war. Beneath the rubble the cellars of this once great house are still intact, though blocked off for safety reasons. Local folklore tells of a terrifying apparition of a woman in white, seen drifting up from the cellar and haunting the ruins of the hall. The same spirit is also said to have been seen in a nearby wooded area, known locally as 'the Vale'. It was here that her appearance terrified a group of Army Cadets on night exercises. One of the cadets, a lad called Mark, was so frightened he could not be persuaded to enter those woods again.

The White Lady is also said to haunt the local quarry, source of the famous Mansfield Woodhouse stone. A white lady, known as Lady Lucy, has been seen at nearby

Shirebrook as well, described again as a ghostly figure in flowing white robes. She is said to frequent the site of the local comprehensive school; apparently her shade became 'earthbound' to this location long before it was a school. Could the same ghost be travelling, or are there two ghosts? Or is this an example of the survival of the folk-memory, through local folklore, of ancient pagan nature deities, metamorphosed as White Lady ghosts?

NEWARK

The Ghost of Caesar's Palace

DURING the autumn and winter of 1994 the Corn Exchange in Castlegate underwent a major refurbishment. At a cost of over £1 million the building was transformed from a bingo hall into a prestigious nightclub named Caesar's Palace. With several bars and a landscaped beer garden overlooking the river Trent, Caesar's Palace has become a popular night spot. However, whilst revellers party the night away their antics may be being watched by a ghost. On the nightclub's first New Year's Eve party, one of the staff took a photograph of the packed dance floor. Although nothing unusual was seen at the time the print shows a misty spectral form floating above the dancers. This was one in a chain of events that have led the staff to believe that Caesar's Palace is haunted.

The Corn Exchange was opened in 1848 to provide a venue for Newark's thriving cereal trade. Built by a con-sortium of millers headed by John Thorpe, the Exchange was designed by the London architect Henry Deusbury.

In 1911 it became 'The Cinematograph Hall' showing early silent movies. The Corn Exchange ceased to function as such in 1914. In the 1920s it was an auction room and dances were held there in World War II. In 1971 it became a bingo hall and it is known that the Exchange was lived in during this period.

The Romanesque columns, arches and statues suggested the new nightclub's name, with the theme of Roman decadence being tastefully developed inside. The ballroom is decorated in gold and black, with mirrored walls. The original balcony has been enhanced to provide more seating with views over the dance floor and second bar. Mr Derek Amos, the Manager, has been closely involved with the refurbishment. It was during the building work that the suggestion of a resident ghost was raised. 'When we were building the place we ripped everything out and it was just a shell. There were noises and one or two of the builders did say they saw something. I stayed here when we were installing the security systems and heard all sorts of noises. We were in the cellar sleeping and heard the noises . . . We searched the place with torches but didn't find any cause. It could have been the wind getting up, we just don't know.

'All the walls were covered from floor to ceiling in this cheap panelling stuff. When we took this off everyone was commenting on what good condition the walls were in. Then, about halfway up, in between where the floor of the balcony is now, this outline started to appear. It was the outline of a person. You could see the head and the shoulders and then it faded out. It didn't have legs. The only way you could have got up there is with a ladder. It wasn't something that someone had drawn on with chalk or something. It wasn't a damp patch. It was a dark brown colour. After a day or two it faded away. It was just an outline. It was there for a couple of nights and then went. It went as mysteriously as it came. Whatever it was is behind the mirrors now.'

Once the club was open for business more strange events followed. Several of the bar staff reported odd things happening in the disco bar. The bar manager, Chris, who has since left the Palace, saw bar mats picked up and dropped by some unseen force. Nicola, another member of staff, witnessed further mischief: 'I always work on the same part of the bar, near the till. This is where I saw glasses fly off the shelf. I was standing here when I heard this glass crash to the floor. I thought nothing of it and swept up the bits. Then another glass fell. The glasses were well back from the edge of the shelf, and we'd been busy so there would have been even fewer glasses there. This has happened several times since, always in the same part of the bar and always the same type of glass, never a pint glass. This always seems to happen when we're busy. It can't be explained by vibrations from the disco, it's a mystery, several of the staff have seen this happen.' Some of the staff have become reluctant to be in the disco bar on their own when it's empty.

Derek Amos paid little attention to his staff's misgivings. Large public buildings are eerie after hours, and it wasn't surprising that in such an old building there should be talk of ghosts. However, his equanimity was to soon disappear. 'It was a Monday night and we'd had about 400 teenagers in. They had all gone. This would be about 10.30 pm. We had locked up everywhere. It was dark. I was locking the office up. I locked the door and I was walking across the balcony when I saw something out of the corner of my eye, near to the bar. I thought at first that it was someone who had been left behind, or hiding behind to rob the place. It was standing between the two central pillars by the balcony rail. As I approached I could see it wasn't human. It was just a misty shape of a person. The eyes seemed to be prominent. I'm not easily frightened, but I ran down the stairs and flew across the dance floor. I looked up and it seemed to move towards the railing around the balcony. I couldn't make out if it was a man or a woman. Then I flew downstairs into the other bar (Capello's) and told the staff what I'd seen. None of them would come to have a look. For my own peace of mind I wanted to have another look, and a girl called Sarah agreed go back up there with me. She definitely saw this thing on the balcony. We went back downstairs for torches and a few more of the staff came up then. We searched the balcony area but there was nothing. A few of the staff say they've seen something since, but I can only say what I saw. Thinking back, this figure wasn't far from where that image appeared on the wall. It was weird. When in the past people have said to me that they've seen a ghost I always thought it was a trick of the light, but now I'm open minded.'

In the *Nottingham Journal* of 7th May 1847 it was reported that: 'The late Mrs Guthrie's house in Castle Gate, overlooking the Trent, has been purchased and is to be demolished for the erection of a covered Corn Exchange on the site, at the instance of Messrs Thorpe and other millers of the town.' Mrs Guthrie had died in 1841 and the house remained empty until it was demolished. Why was it left unoccupied? Was it haunted? The house was described as a 'dwelling of some pretensions and a rather handsome exterior. It was set back...from the street and had a small plot of grass and a garden in front, the whole house and grounds being enclosed with a massive iron palisade and gates. Further out, between the causeway and the road, were five or six mature trees.' Could Mrs Guthrie be the ghost that haunts Caesar's Palace? Or is the resident spectre of a more recent origin? Whatever the case, those customers dancing the night away should spare a thought for the staff who must make ready the club after hours, in the silence and the dark.

NEWSTEAD ABBEY

The Newstead Eagle and the Sunken Treasure

THE monastic house of Newstead Abbey was founded by the Augustinian monks in the 12th century. The abbey became the ancestral home of the Byron family after Sir John Byron of Colwick was given the house and lands by Henry VIII in 1540. Today, Newstead is most famous for having been the home of the 6th Lord Byron, George Gordon, 'Byron the poet'. George Gordon loved Newstead and all the legends and mystery associated with the abbey.

The story of the brass eagle lectern that stands in the nave of Southwell Minster is unique. Similar lecterns can be seen in many of the cathedrals of Europe, but this one lay hidden for 200 years at the bottom of a lake at

Newstead. After this remarkable find the lake was named 'The Eagle pond'; it lies in sight of Devil's Wood on the eastern side of the abbey. According to legend, the lectern was carefully hidden in the waters along with far greater treasure at the time of the Dissolution of the Monasteries. King Henry VIII wanted to be the supreme spiritual and temporal power in the realm, and at the same time to fill his depleted Treasury. The Suppression Act of 1536, therefore, transferred all monastic buildings, land, goods and chattels to the Crown and Henry took many priceless religious treasures for himself. Even the lead from the roofs was plundered, hastening the collapse into ruin of some of Europe's finest medieval buildings. Legend has it that in this atmosphere of impending doom a boat put out onto the dark water of the lake at Newstead Abbey. On board were several monks, the abbot himself, the great brass eagle lectern and a vast iron chest containing the gold and silver treasure of the abbey, accumulated over generations.

The lectern was found in the time of the 5th Lord Byron, in about 1740. It had apparently suffered little damage from its concealment in the lake and it was sold to an antiquities dealer in Nottingham. As it was being cleaned and restored, the lectern's secret was revealed. The brass eagle stands on a globe which surmounts a column. When the eagle was removed from its perch the globe and column were found to be hollow. Inside were ancient parchments perfectly intact, the property deeds and other vital documents relating to Newstead Abbey. The abbot had intended to retrieve these later from their hiding place in the hope of restoring the abbey to its rightful owners. Less noble in sentiment were the ready-made indulgences said to be found together with the deeds. These were essentially 'forgiveness in advance' for any sins committed in the meantime. These documents would have been of enormous interest to scholars, but they were burnt by the dealer. The lectern was later purchased by Sir Richard Kaye, Prebendary of North Muskham and Dean of Lincoln, who presented it to Southwell Minster in 1805, where it remains to this day. But what of the treasure?

Washington Irving (1783–1859), the American author, stayed at the house and recorded the visit in his book

Abbotsford and Newstead Abbey. Here he retells the story of the eagle lectern and the sunken treasure. According to Irving, the treasure is in an iron chest of huge dimensions, with an iron loop at each end. He mentions a local tale that the chest was once seen, emerging from the water, during a period of unusually severe drought. Other accounts tell how ropes were attached to the great iron loops and horses were used from the shore to pull at the chest, but it wouldn't budge. Some say this is due to the huge amounts of gold and silver, chalices, crosses and other jewel-encrusted items weighing it down. Irving says that a second, supernatural, reason was offered for the chest's immovability, a curse or spell had been placed on it by the monks. Eventually a man was put into the shallow water but the soft mud of the lake floor offered no purchase, indeed the mud threatened to suck the man down and drown him. All attempts failed, no means were found to secure the chest. It rained heavily and the waters of the lake rose. No one had thought to attach a buoy to mark the chest's position and it disappeared beneath the waters once more. All efforts to find the treasure since have proved fruitless. Despite being hounded by his creditors, the 5th Lord is said to have paid a man 14 shillings and eightpence to excavate around the abbey grounds searching for treasure; none was found. One of the guides at Newstead took the opportunity some years ago, whilst the Eagle pond had been drained, to use a metal detector on the muddy bottom – he was rewarded by finding a rusty pistol and some bullets, but no treasure.

On 22nd March 1966, two-and-a-half miles from Newstead, one of the largest hoards of jewellery and medieval coins ever found in England was unearthed on a building site. Some 1,237 gold coins were found at Fishpool, in Ravenshead, on the junction between Summercourt Drive and Cambourne Gardens. They were dated between 1351 and 1464 and are now in the British Museum collection. The origin of the hoard remains unknown, but the site on which it was found lies between two ancient roads to Nottingham and near the old route between Newstead and Blidworth. The dates on the coins are well before the Dissolution of the Monasteries.

However, this in itself does not rule out the Fishpool hoard as monastic treasure; the coins could have been hidden long after they were minted. Is this hoard the source of the legend of Newstead's lost treasure?

Byron and the Ghosts of Newstead Abbey

GEORGE GORDON, 6th Baron Byron of Rochdale, was born in London in 1788. He was the only son of the eccentric Captain John 'Mad Jack' Byron (1756–91) and Catherine Gordon of Gight, Aberdeen. George Gordon had a poor start. Born lame, he spent the first ten years of his life in his mother's lodgings in Aberdeen, his father having abandoned his wife and child after squandering her fortune in France. In 1798 he succeeded to the title on the death of his great-uncle, 'the Wicked Lord'. With his creditors pressing, George Gordon married Anne Isabella Milbanke, an heiress, in 1815. Anne left him following the birth of their daughter Ada, the rift being due to Byron's more than brotherly love for his half-sister, Augusta Leigh, and other misdemeanours. The resulting scandal forced Byron into exile in Europe. After many adventures he died in Greece in 1824.

Shortly before his disastrous marriage, Byron encountered the Black Friar of Newstead Abbey. This ghost, also known as the 'Goblin Friar', was said to appear to the head of the Byron family before any unhappy event. The poet vividly recalls this meeting in his poem *Don Juan* (canto XVI), in which he records:

> . . . but lo! a monk, arrayed
> In cowl and beads, and dusky garb, appear'd,
> Now in the moonlight, and now lapsed in shade,
> With steps that trod as heavy, yet unheard;
> His garments only a slight murmur made;
> He moved as shadowy as the Sisters weird,
> But slowly; and as he pass'd Juan by,
> Glanced, without pausing, on him a bright eye.

According to Washington Irving, the author of the

famous American ghost story *Legend of Sleepy Hollow*, Lord Byron had several supernatural experiences in a bedchamber known as the Rook Cell, where the poet described having been woken by the sensation of something mounting the bed. On sitting up he was confronted by a shapeless black mass, featureless apart from two red, glowing eyes. The apparition rolled from the bed onto the floor and disappeared. Lord Byron is also said to have seen a mysterious column of white vapour rising from the floor, which vanished without a trace. The poet was fond of ghost stories, and enjoyed the exquisite chill they can bring to the spine. When he and the Shelleys stayed together at Lake Leman in Switzerland, Byron suggested the party tell each other ghost stories. Mary Shelley rose to his challenge and created Frankenstein's monster, the most enduring Gothic horror story of all.

Washington Irving himself slept in the Rook Cell when staying at Newstead with the then owner, Colonel Wildman. It is still furnished today as the poet had left it, and well worth a visit. The room takes its name from an ancient rookery in the abbey grounds that it overlooks. Irving noted with interest that each morning the rooks would wake as a body and fly away en masse, in formation, to sweep the countryside for food; they would return in similar manner in the evening, where their discussion of the day's events would echo around the estate. Irving was told that the rooks at Newstead observed the Sabbath – they set out every day except Sunday, when they stayed in the abbey grounds. He didn't believe this until he saw it for himself. Indeed it appeared that the rooks visited their neighbours and friends, devoting Sunday to their nearest and dearest but not leaving the estate. Irving tells us that local tradition had it that the rooks at Newstead were the souls of the Black Monks, reborn as birds, still occupying their old abbey. Indeed so strongly was this belief held that, contrary to common country practice, the Newstead rooks were not shot and were generally left unhindered.

The Skull Goblet

HEAVILY in debt and pursued by his creditors, like the 5th Lord before him, Byron the poet undertook a treasure hunt at Newstead. Even after extensive excavations all that was found was a human skull, presumably that of a monk. Byron, however, was delighted with the find and had it sent to a Nottingham jeweller to be made into a goblet. Worrying not a jot about incurring further debt, Byron had the skull mounted on a stem and base of silver and polished up with a gold trim around the rim, where the lips would meet the cup. The goblet is said to have held nearly a full bottle of wine and was amongst his favourite things. It had pride of place at the poet's frequent parties and was a great talking point amongst his guests.

After the poet's death the goblet became a treasured relic of his life at Newstead, that is until Ethel Webb took exception to it. On the death of Colonel Thomas Wildman, Newstead was bought by William Frederick Webb, a wealthy landowner, in 1861 and much restoration and refurbishment was carried out by the Webb family in subsequent years. Towards the end of the 19th century the Webb sisters, Geraldine and Ethel, extensively altered the gardens, Ethel creating the Japanese Garden in 1907. Ethel appears to have been the epitome of the respectable 'Edwardian Lady'. A pious Christian, she did not share Byron's macabre tastes and no deference to the poet's memory could overcome her loathing of the skull goblet. On Ethel's instruction, Canon Barber, the Webb family's minister, gave the skull a Christian burial at a secret location in the grounds. Whether Ethel had the silver stem removed beforehand is unknown, but it seems highly likely she would have had it melted down.

So a unique artefact was lost – but not forgotten. A group of Byron devotees, known as the 'Monks' (Members of Newstead Kindred Society), commissioned a replica of the skull goblet to be made. From a surviving picture of the original a facsimile was crafted by Joanne Pond, silversmith of the Longdale Craft Centre at Ravenshead. Though a replica, the bowl of the new skull cup is made from a real human skull and lined with silver. Very appropriately, the cost of the replica was met with funds raised via a series of 'ghost evenings'. In July 1994, with all due ceremony, the goblet was presented to the Sheriff of Nottingham, Councillor Ronald MacIntosh, by one of the 'Monks', dressed as the Black Friar for the occasion. The skull goblet now has pride of place as part of the Byron collection, a tribute to a great romantic hero and one of our finest poets.

Mother Shipton and the Byrons of Newstead

WILLIAM, the 5th Lord Byron, known as 'the Wicked Lord', was eccentric to say the least. The epitome of the 'Mad Byrons', he was found guilty of manslaughter by the House of Lords after killing a cousin in a drunken brawl. After paying costs, he was released and retired from the world to Newstead. William cared little for the opinions of others. He took one of the household servants, Mrs Hardstaffe, as his mistress – his wife having deserted him after he shot dead her coachman. Needless to say, he was not well loved by his tenants. It is believed he deliberately allowed the estate to fall into decay to spite his son and heir, who had married against his wishes. William pursued his own pleasures furiously. It was said that wild orgies, lasting days, took place regularly at Newstead. Indeed, it was in the pursuit of a whim that the 5th Lord Byron fulfilled a prophecy, and brought about the end of the Byrons at Newstead.

Old Mother Shipton was a prophetess and revered as a fortune teller. We are told she was born in 1486 and died 165 years later in 1651. She is said to have predicted such momentous events as the Great Fire of London in 1666, the invention of the motor car, telecommunications and air travel. In the form of rhymes, her prophesies became famous the length of the land. In one prediction she stated that when a ship loaded with 'ling' sailed across Sherwood Forest, Newstead Abbey would pass out of the Byron family for ever. Ling is an Old Norse word for heather, and it appears as a local place-name – Ling Forest near Mansfield.

William loved to stage mock naval battles on the Upper

Lake at Newstead. He built castles on each side of the lake, fitted out with miniature cannons. He is said to have particularly enjoyed the fright that the loud explosions gave to his neighbours. 'The Wicked Lord's' miniature fleet was crewed by his servants; and whilst none are recorded as being killed, they must have been in some peril as he took his pleasure in blowing up the ships with cannonfire from the lake shore. Not content with this, William sent for a larger vessel, a 20-gun schooner. The ship was brought all the way from the coast, across land and through Sherwood Forest, to be launched on the lake. This caused great excitement amongst the ordinary people, excitement and indeed resentment. Old Mother Shipton's prediction was remembered. Word quickly spread and as the ship made its stately way through the forest heather was thrown onto her decks as she passed. By the time it reached Newstead the ship was truly laden with 'ling'.

The 5th Lord Byron's response to this is not recorded, but William probably found it amusing. However, the 'Mad Byrons' were soon depleted. 'The Wicked Lord's' grandson became heir to the Newstead estate, then died young in Corsica. William's brother, a Vice Admiral known as 'Foul Weather Jack' from his uncanny ability to attract storms whenever he was at sea, died in 1786. 'Foul Weather' had disinherited his own son 'Mad Jack'. Following a scandalous affair 'Mad Jack' married the ex-wife of the Marquis of Carmarthen. This ended in tragedy when she died giving birth to their daughter, Augusta. 'Mad Jack' then married for money. Having squandered his new wife's fortune and fathered George Gordon, 'Mad Jack' died in 1790, 'penniless, poxed and unrepentant'. 'The Wicked Lord' outlived them all. William spent his last days in the kitchen, the only warm room, with a sound roof, now left in the ruined abbey. For company he had his tame crickets, which came to his call and fed from his hand. William finally died in May 1798. The crickets are said to have left en masse, as did the few remaining servants. George Gordon, William's great nephew, whom he had called 'the lame brat', inherited title and estate.

When George Gordon became the 6th Baron he was ten years old. The estate was no longer financially viable, indeed it had been plundered. Trees had been cut down for timber and an auction of June 1778 had emptied Newstead of the family heirlooms, the furniture, silver, plate and china. Byron the poet, as he became, loved Newstead. He took up residence in 1808 in those parts of the abbey that were still habitable, his friend Francis Hodgson describing the poet's quarters as 'so comfortably appointed . . . and cheerful with capacious fires made one forget that one was domiciled in the wing of an extensive ruin.' However, despite his best attempts, Byron was forced to sell the estate. The abbey was bought by Colonel Wildman in 1817 for £94,000. Debt, both inherited and accumulated, made the poet 'the last Byron of Newstead'. As Samuel Pepys wrote after the Great Fire of London, 'Shipton's prophesy is out'.

NOTTINGHAM

The Adams Building Ghost

OF all the buildings in Nottingham's famous Lace Market the Adams Building is the most imposing. A mixture of Italian and Renaissance styles, rising to six storeys, it looms above Stoney Street, looking more like a grand mansion than a purpose built factory. This was the premises of Thomas Adams, Page and Co. The factory was divided into 14 departments making all types of lace and net. When it was opened, 'with good ceremony', in 1855 the architect, T. C. Hine of London, was criticised for making the building too grand for its use. However, the philanthropic Thomas Adams wanted a factory that expressed all his deeply held evangelical principles. This was to be no 'dark satanic mill'. There was a dining room, a men's tearoom, a library, a classroom and a chapel, which the workers were paid to attend every morning. By 1858, 500 people worked here, with a similar number of outworkers employed about the town.

Despite the laudable conditions created by Thomas Adams, a ghost has found cause to haunt the building. Over many years factory workers have reported seeing the spectral figure of a woman in a long dress gliding amidst the sewing machines and offices. It isn't known who the ghost was or why she haunts this building. Like so many vast Victorian factories, today the Adams Building is divided up into smaller units. On the first floor is the Mary Adams lingerie workshop, where the ghost of a woman has been seen several times in the reception office. The receptionist, Diane Lovett, has not seen the ghost herself but has often felt a presence in the room, as if she were being watched. She does, however, know of others who have. Diane Wooley, a supervisor at the factory, saw the ghost in the reception area and mistook it for the receptionist, only to realise her mistake as the figure vanished before her. Should the staff at Mary Adams wish to be rid of the ghost they should look no further than the basement units. Mr Julian Holland of Bridal Laces and Fabrics, below the Adams Building, is a dowser and ex-chairman of the East Midlands Dowsing Group. Amongst his talents for detecting water, minerals and lost property, Julian can pick up on the presence of ghosts. As he puts it, 'Ghosts are spirits who are where they shouldn't be so you can act as a kind of traffic policeman and send them on their way.'

Nottingham Castle

NOTTINGHAM CASTLE has had a long and chequered career. Sitting high up on an outcrop of sandstone, it occupies a natural defensive position but only the restored gatehouse and some foundations now remain of the Norman castle built around 1068. During the 'Anarchy of King Stephen' it was destroyed and rebuilt twice. In 1313 a band of the townspeople attacked the king's yeomanry in the castle and killed the Mayor. In the affray one of the rebels was captured and imprisoned in the castle until he was freed by a comrade who secretly gained entrance – echoes of Robin Hood? In 1335 there was another revolt, the castle gates were breached and the castle itself was besieged for eight days. King Charles I raised the Stuart standard at the castle at the beginning of the English Civil War, but it ominously blew away that night in a storm. After the defeat of the Royalists the castle, like so many others, was 'slighted' on the orders of Cromwell and a fine baroque mansion took its place, built between 1674 and 1679 by the Duke of Newcastle. This house was completely gutted by fire in the Reform Bill riots of 1831 and remained a ruin until 1875. It was rescued by the Nottingham Corporation, and was restored and refurbished as the city's art gallery and museum. Despite its disappointing un-castle-like appearance, especially for those visitors seeking the romance of Robin Hood, the building has had both drama and mystery aplenty.

The castle is thoroughly haunted and beneath its rocky foundations are tunnels and secret passages. Underneath it, carved into the sandstone outcrop on which it stands, is the famous tunnel known as Mortimer's Hole. The passageway is eerie enough, made all the more so by the reputed presence of the ghost of Sir Roger Mortimer himself. Mortimer, the Earl of March and lover of Queen Isabel, was probably her accomplice in the murder of Edward II. On the night of 19th October 1330 the Queen and her lover were staying at Nottingham Castle. Seeking to bring his father's killer to justice and expose his feckless mother, the young King Edward III entered the network of secret tunnels that led ultimately into the castle itself. With a band of loyal supporters, the King burst into his mother's bedroom and surprised the lovers. Edward himself is said to have seized Mortimer. The now doomed regicide was led away, so legend has it, to Isabel's mournful cries of 'Fair son, have pity on the gentle Mortimer'. Sir Roger was imprisoned in the castle, then taken to London and executed as a traitor at Tyburn. He was hanged, drawn and quartered on the 29th November 1330 and his wretched remains skewered on spikes and left to rot on Traitors' Gate. The tunnel that led to Sir Roger's downfall became known after him. The castle's tunnels, as well as the extensive system of passages under the city, are open to the public and well worth a visit.

There are other ghosts connected with the castle. In 1212

King John held some 28 sons of Welsh noble families hostage there. The boys, some as young as twelve, lived at the castle for some time, and were allowed free rein within the walls, then one day, the precise date is unknown, King John ordered that all the hostages should be executed. A chronicler states that the boys' pitiful cries rang around the castle as one after the other they were taken up on the ramparts and hanged in a row. Their ghostly pleas for mercy are still said to be heard within the castle precincts. In a newspaper article on the castle that appeared in the 1920s an elderly resident of Nottingham told of his boyhood home in Castle Gate that was plagued by ghosts. It was believed by his family that they were haunted by ghosts from the castle itself. How or why the ghosts 'went over the wall' was never explained and the haunting stopped as quickly as it started. There are also old accounts of the ghostly sounds of billiard balls clicking late at night at Newdigate House in Castle Gate. Phantom voices and footsteps heard in the entrance hall further suggest that the house is haunted.

The Trip to Jerusalem

REPUTED to be the oldest pub in England, the Trip to Jerusalem is thought to have been built in 1189. It was a favourite watering hole for the crusaders on their way to the Holy Land and Richard the Lionheart is said to have stayed here on one of his brief stops in England. The word 'Trip' or 'Trypp' comes, we are told, from an old word for halt or stop. Much of the fabric of the building is carved out from the rock on which the castle above stands and the walls and ceilings are bedecked with all manner of curios and antiques, some dating back to the Civil War. The lighting casts weird shadows about, and the Trip has an atmosphere to which written description cannot do justice – it must be experienced. Patrick Dare and his wife Marilyn became managers of the pub in February 1994. Marilyn knows much of the pub's strange history and has had weird experiences there of her own.

In the Rock Lounge is a model galleon hanging from the

ceiling, covered by what looks like 50 years of dust and cobwebs. No one will clean the galleon because it is cursed. According to Marilyn, 'The last three people who have cleaned it are said to have died mysterious and unexpected deaths within twelve months of doing so.' The model is the largest of several hanging from the ceiling. They are thought to be parting gifts from sailors who had made them to pass the time at sea, like the scrimshaw of the whalers. Nottingham was once a busy inland port, the river Trent being navigable for quite large vessels all the way to the Humber and the North Sea. The maker of this particular model is unknown but it is completely shrouded in dust-thickened cobwebs. No name is visible on the galleon's side, and it would be a foolhardy soul that would wipe away the dust to find one. The Rock Lounge in particular seems to be a focal point for odd happenings. Things such as keys disappear only to turn up later in odd places. Glasses and bottles have been known to fly off the shelves and smash, when no one is near by. Staff have heard the sound of breaking glass coming from the bar, but when they've gone with a dustpan and brush to clear it up, they simply can't find any. Sometimes a waft of perfume fills the air, which Marilyn describes as old-fashioned scent, like lavender or rose water.

Marilyn and Patrick were informed that the pub was haunted when they arrived. 'We were told that a group of tourists had asked to see the cellars and they saw two foot-soldiers walk through a wall. This was seen by the whole party, a group of five people. A medium visited the pub and she told us that a clock hanging in the bar was possessed by two evil spirits. A previous landlady had two Dobermanns that hated that clock. They would stand and bark at it for no reason. Our Dobermann, Moritz, named after Baron von Richthofen's deerhound, howled whenever we put him in the office, he still doesn't like being shut in there. This is an entrance to Mortimer's Hole and they say animals are very sensitive to atmosphere. Previous landlords have both seen and heard two ghosts, a man and a woman. We hear people calling when there's no one there. The woman, wearing what appears to be crinoline skirts, is seen walking down the stairs into the cellars.'

Carved out from the soft rock, the cellars of the Trip to Jerusalem are like interconnecting caves. They have been in use at least since the Norman Conquest and probably longer. A narrow shaft pierces the rock above all the way up to the castle. It is believed this was a 'shouting hole' to allow those in the castle to call for more ale from the cellars below. In one chamber in the cellars a horseshoe-shaped bench has been cut into the rock around the walls; this was a cockfighting pit. According to Marilyn, 'Sometimes you can smell tallow burning down there. They used this for candles. The smell can linger for 20 minutes and then it's suddenly gone.'

On the far side of the cellars a rusting iron gate hangs limply from its hinges before a doorway cut into the rock wall. This is said to be the condemned cell of the castle prison. A curious green mould grows on the walls and ceiling. A rock bench has been carved out on one wall, offering cold comfort to the unfortunate inmates. The condemned cell isn't used to store beer as the ceiling is too low; for the most part it is kept empty. There is something more to the cell's oppressive atmosphere than its natural chill – there is a palpable cloud of doom here. Marilyn concurs with this, 'As you walk in the cell, you know it's not right, you know it is evil. Men condemned to death were shackled to the walls in there. Some left to die of starvation or dehydration. Two of the pub's regulars, full of Dutch courage, once decided they would spend the night in the condemned cell. They lasted 20 minutes, and were violently sick afterwards. My husband had some eerie experiences down there, not long after we'd moved in. The mallets for tapping the barrels kept disappearing. These are big rubber ones that are always kept in the same place. Sometimes you go down there and you can't find one anywhere, only to look again to see three mallets lined up on three consecutive barrels, where you've just looked. One day he needed to get something from the other side of the cellar. He didn't bother to turn the light on and as he crossed the room something icy touched him lightly on the back of his neck. Needless to say the lights are always on now if anyone is working in there.

'Sometime later I was working at the sink, near the

condemned cell, washing some buckets out, when I saw something walk past me. There was no one else there and it couldn't have been a shadow, it was like a grey mass. I had this feeling like an icy bar being passed through my body. I just stood there totally still. Then I looked at my feet because I felt this iciness come down and go out through my toes and I shuddered from head to foot. I don't know whether it was a condemned prisoner that hasn't passed over properly, or a soul in torment but it was a totally evil feeling, horrible. I wouldn't go down there again for about three weeks. It really frightened me.'

OLLERTON

The New Ollerton Ghosts

OLLERTON is divided into two halves, Old Ollerton, going back to Domesday, and New Ollerton, built to house the colliers and their families when the mine was opened. The two halves of the town have their own histories and identities, and their own ghosts.

New Ollerton has a clutch of ghosts centred, not surprisingly, around the mine and the colliers' houses. The owners of a beautifully restored cottage on Cinder Lane had the unusual experience of seeing half a ghost in December 1993 in their home. The ghost, seen again since, seems to be the upper torso of a man, just like a marble bust, and is an unearthly blue colour. It floats through the downstairs area of the house, apparently oblivious to the present living residents. It first appeared when a fireplace was knocked out and replaced with a fashionable wood-burning stove.

Near the entrance to the colliery are some Victorian cottages, haunted by an old man in one property and the ghost of a crying child. The cottages' precise location is not given, at the request of residents to protect their properties' value. The old man's ghost seems quite benign; he appears in what was the back kitchen of the house and seems to go back and forth to the sink. Perhaps he was making tea when he died and the event has become frozen in time. The ghost of the crying child is quite different. Several residents in the past have been disturbed by the pitiful crying of a child both inside and outside the cottages. Everything from cats and mating hedgehogs, to wind in the chimneys has been suggested as a cause, but those who have heard it have definitely said it is a crying child. The sound seems to focus on one house in particular but whenever a search has been made no cause has been found. Sometimes it is a low sobbing, at others a despairing wailing. One resident moved from the area because of the distress caused by this mournful noise. Whatever dreadful sorrow the child endured is a mystery but its spirit, it seems, remains comfortless still.

The road between Ollerton and Edwinstowe has long been an accident blackspot. The entrance to Thoresby Colliery is about midway between the two villages and heavy lorries travel to and from the pit on this road. Often the surface is made slippery by coal dust and muck washed down from the tip. Drivers need to take extra care here for, in addition to the occasionally hazardous conditions, this road is haunted. Some people have reported that a cyclist suddenly appears out of nowhere in front of them, leaving them no time to avoid a collision. Yet, as they brace themselves for the impact, the rider seems to pass straight through their vehicle. Those that have stopped to investigate have found nothing, no injured man, no crushed cycle, nothing. In the early 1960s a pit worker from Ollerton was killed on this stretch of road one dark autumn day. The man was Polish and had come to Britain during the war. On the day he died it had been raining and it has been suggested that his cyclist's raincoat had obscured his rear lights. Despite the fact that this tragedy happened so many years ago, the same man is still seen cycling to work, especially on wet autumnal days. Drivers are advised to watch out!

The Ollerton Hall Ghost

OLLERTON HALL was built in about 1640 by Thomas Markham. Thomas had the old manor house pulled down to build the hall which was one of the finest houses in Nottinghamshire, with an impressive panelled 'parlour dining room, ornamented with carving and intricate scroll work'. The hall is one of the earliest brick buildings in the county. Sadly, it has never prospered and it has remained empty for most of this century, an empty shell with boarded up windows. It has been earmarked for some time for conversion to a children's home, but as yet no work has begun. The hall's air of gloom and decay has more to it than simply that of an abandoned house. Ollerton Hall is haunted by the wandering ghost of Colonel Markham himself.

Colonel Markham fought for the King in the English Civil War and was killed at the battle of Gainsborough. In his book *Ollerton B. C. – Before the Colliery*, D. J. Bradbury tells of Sir Thomas Markham's part in the Civil War and of the stories surrounding his death: 'Thomas Markham was an early supporter of the Royalist cause. He became a colonel in General Charles Cavendish's cavalry and played a significant part in the battles of Grantham and Stamford. There are conflicting accounts of what happened next. One story says that he was present when Cavendish was killed at Gainsborough and led the Royalist forces in an orderly retreat, but was himself killed a few days later at Horncastle. However, the battle of Gainsborough took place on 31 July, while the parish register of Ollerton states that he died on 22 July. The local tradition about his death is that he and his men were driven into the marshland by the River Trent near Gainsborough (presumably before the main battle) and that Markham drowned there.'

Tradition has it that his body was brought back to the hall and laid out in an empty chamber on the north side of the house, distinguishable from the outside by an oddly shaped window in a recess. It was reached by some wooden stairs that ran down into the kitchen. In due course the body was buried in the village church. However, Colonel Markham's spirit did not rest easy. The servants of the house were soon disturbed by the heavy tread of footsteps on the back stairs when no one at all was there to cause them. The shade of Colonel Markham was not confined to the hall. He was seen at several places around Ollerton – at the corner of the road leading to Physics Row, on the back lane near the old Free School and on the bridge across the river. His favourite haunt was on the Edwinstowe road at a spot known as Cockglode Green. This is all that survives from what were once the manicured gardens of Cockglode House, which was near the present day entrance to Thoresby Colliery. You can still see the acacia, lime trees, and sprawling rhododendrons of Cockglode Green thriving on the heathland, amidst the birch and gorse. Here, after dark, the ghost was the terror of travellers and courting couples alike.

An account of the Ollerton Hall ghost appeared in the *Retford and Gainsborough Times* on 27th March 1903. As well as lamenting the sorry state of the hall, the article recounts several disturbing instances involving the ghost that occurred at the turn of the century. At that time Ollerton had a tannery. Builders were engaged to build a brick drying chamber over some pickling vats containing a mixture of water and lime in which the hides were cured. A bricklayer and carpenter were on a platform above these vats in the process of lowering a heavy beam into position to support the floor of the drying chamber. Without any warning, some unseen force grabbed hold of the beam and threw it and the two men into the pickling vat below. As they climbed out, covered in lime, the workers were terrified to see standing before them the ghost of Colonel Markham. The ghost spoke to them, but neither man would ever reveal what it said. However, the experience changed their lives forever, one becoming a committed churchgoer, and the other a devout spiritualist.

Another worker at the tannery was also attacked by the ghost. A man called Jimmy met the ghost one night under some fir trees on Back Lane. According to the account in the newspaper, the ghost was huge, much bigger than a man. Despite this, Jimmy fought with it. He was found the next morning lying unconscious in the lane, covered in mud, with his hair sticking up on end. It was said that no amount of hair oil could make Jimmy's hair lie flat again.

The tannery workers were not the only ones to feel the wrath of the Colonel's ghost. A plumber and glazier, returning late one night from a dinner at Edwinstowe, met him at Cockglode Green. The ghost was in full uniform, and appeared to be headless. It again attacked the men. They were both thrown to the ground with terrific strength and left bruised and battered. One of the men apparently never stayed out late again.

A local policeman had not only his career but his health permanently ruined by the Ollerton Hall ghost. On one occasion the constable met the spectre at a hop kiln that stood on Forest Side. The ghost beckoned him and he followed – it led him straight into the river, where he almost drowned. On the road where the old toll bar stood he again met the ghost, and again it motioned to him to follow it. This time the policeman attempted to arrest the ghost, only to be dealt with like the others who had stood up to it. He was thrown into some thick gorse bushes and badly scratched, lying there until help came from the nearby toll house. The policeman never recovered from his ordeal. He left the force following the last incident and is said to have died soon after this, his health severely impaired by his traumatic experiences. There have been no other reports about the ghost in local newspapers since this time. However, the hall has been empty so long that it could still be wandering around in the vacant rooms, unnoticed.

Mrs Jones and the Snooty Fox

THE Snooty Fox in Old Ollerton is a 17th-century pub with all the character and appeal of a real English country hostelry. A freehouse with excellent wines, real ale and a sumptuous menu on offer, it is well worth a visit after a day out in Sherwood Forest. It is also haunted. Mr David Slinger bought the pub in November 1991 and soon learnt from the incumbent manager and his wife of the resident ghost. The couple said that a figure of a middle-aged woman appeared in the private accommodation of the pub and that eerie noises were often heard about the place. Mrs Jones, as the ghost is known locally, is said to have haunted the building for centuries. This couple soon left for pastures new and a new manager, Mr Lindsey Andrews, took over.

He was a single man and lived alone on the premises. However, the appearance of Mrs Jones soon ended his solitude. Shortly after moving in, Mr Andrews had the unnerving experience of finding Mrs Jones at the foot of his bed. The ghost was seen frequently by Mr Andrews and became such a cause of concern to him that he raised the matter with the pub's owner, Mr Slinger. The vicar of the parish was consulted. The Rev David Perret visited the private apartments where the ghost had been seen and was of the opinion that there was indeed a presence there. His impression was that the ghost only put in an appearance at the pub when the inhabitants were under some stress or difficulty. He performed a 'blessing' on the pub and no further sightings of Mrs Jones were reported.

Mr Andrews left the Snooty Fox in August 1992 and a temporary manager and his wife took over. They too were troubled by the appearance of Mrs Jones and by unearthly noises around the place. The owner, somewhat preoccupied with finding a new permanent manager for his business, chose, in his own words, to 'ignore their cries'. This couple left soon after. The present hosts of the Snooty Fox, Julian and Elaine, came to the pub in January 1993 and have, so far, been untroubled by Mrs Jones.

Who was the ghost, and why does she haunt the pub? All research into the background of this story has, to date, proved fruitless. No accounts of any tragedy or disaster on the premises have come to light. The parish registers, the census returns and even the index to the tombstones in the churchyard have no entry for a Mrs Jones, although it is possible that the death of a servant or maid at the pub could have been overlooked by history and no record made. The story of the Snooty Fox's ghost, it seems, remains a mystery.

RETFORD

The Elms Hotel Ghost

ON 6th October 1994 an article concerning the Elms Hotel appeared in the local newspaper, the *Retford and Gainsborough Times*. An old soldier had written to the Retford branch of the British Legion, who in turn had contacted the paper. The soldier had been a member of the Field Ambulance Unit and had been billeted at the Elms during the war when it was an unoccupied private house. He was given guard duty on his first night there. At about midnight he went round to the front of the house, where he saw something on the lawn. It appeared to be the ghost of an elderly lady in a long black dress and Victorian-style bonnet. The apparition emerged from behind some bushes to his right, glided across the lawn in front of him and disappeared on the drive to his left. Through fear of ridicule he didn't mention this incident to his comrades. In the 1950s the soldier returned to the Elms with his wife and another couple. By then it was a pub and, the day being hot, offered a welcome opportunity of a drink. However, both the ladies in the party began to shiver and asked to leave the 'creepy' atmosphere. About 15 years after this he again returned to the Elms to find it was now a hotel. Without mentioning his own wartime experience, he learnt from a barmaid that the hotel was haunted by the ghost of an old lady.

Following the original article more letters arrived at the newspaper detailing other reports of the ghost at the Elms Hotel. Mrs Elsie Bacon of Holly Road, Retford, recounted her husband's ghostly experience some years before: 'My husband had been weeding the garden one late afternoon. I was in the kitchen making a cup of tea, I took the tea out to him and he was sat down on the conservatory step as white as a sheet. I asked him what was wrong and he replied that I wouldn't believe it if he told me. He said he felt a presence and looked to one side and three feet away he saw a woman for a few seconds and then she disappeared.' According to Mr Bacon, the ghost had no face. The description of the ghost seen by the ex-soldier matched exactly that of the apparition seen by her husband. Later Mr and Mrs Bacon did some investigation of their own: 'We have since been told that where we live on Holly Road once used to be fields that a long time ago had a pathway, along which an old lady used to carry pails each day. I wonder if that old lady was making her way to the Elms each day.' Another resident, Mr A. H. Smith, remembers that his mother, who was a maid at the house before it was a hotel, often told him of a ghost she'd seen in a nearby spinney.

Devilish Practices on St Mark's Eve

FROM the Nottingham Archdeaconry Papers comes this account of necromancy. On 26th July 1608, Katherine Foxegale, of Walesby, was brought before the church court at Retford, 'For a daylie scolde & curser of her neighbours and for watchinge uppon Sainte Markes even at nighte laste in the Church porche to presage by divelishe demonstracion the deathe of somme neighbours within this yeere.' The record does not show if this took place at St Swithun's church in Retford or at the Norman church of St Edmund at Walesby.

The practice of watching on St Mark's Eve was widespread. From Brand's *Antiquities*, published in 1813, comes this account: 'It is customary in Yorkshire, as a clergyman of that county informed me, for the common people to sit and watch in the church porch on St Mark's Eve (24th April) from eleven o'clock at night until one in the morning. The Third year (for this must be done thrice), they are supposed to see the ghosts of all those who are to die the next year, pass by into the church. When anyone sickens that is thought to have been seen in this manner, it is presently whispered about that he will not recover, for that such, or such an one, who has watched St Mark's Eve, says so.'

Watching on St Mark's Eve was not without its dangers. Henderson's *Northern Counties*, of 1866, spells out the risks:

'I have heard . . . of an old woman at Scarborough, who kept St Mark's vigil in the porch of St Mary's in that town about eighty years ago. Figure after figure glided in the church, turning round to her as they went in . . . At last a figure turned and gazed at her; she knew herself and fell senseless . . . She did not long survive the shock.'

RUFFORD

The Abbey Ghosts

RUFFORD ABBEY is in the heart of Sherwood Forest, and is an absolute must for anyone visiting the area. After the Norman Conquest William I gave the Manor of Rugeford to his own nephew, Gilbert Le Gaunt. Gilbert's grandson Gilbert, Earl of Lincoln, founded a Cistercian abbey at Rufford in 1146. After Henry VIII's Dissolution of the Monasteries the abbey became a private estate; first as the home of the Talbot family, then, in 1626, passing to the Savilles, who lived there for over 300 years until it was sold in 1938. The County Council purchased the abbey ruins and surrounding parkland in 1951 and opened it as a country park in 1969. Rufford Country Park has extensive areas of woodland, including several Sites of Special Scientific Interest, a lake and bird sanctuary, and its own flock of rare Mouflon sheep.

Just beyond the ornate gateway to the abbey grounds is the Rose Cottage pub. This has long had the reputation of being haunted. Mr and Mrs Hurt had many strange experiences when they ran it. Mr Hurt remembers: 'Many times we found cutlery on the lawn, and on one occasion a lamp. They had obviously come from upstairs and we did find a window open. Things were often moved, and we'd hear all kinds of strange noises. One of our waitresses once took an order for coffee from an old man, when she turned to ask him if he wanted anything else he had disappeared. I myself saw flashing lights, like lightning, around a closed door and a cracking sound. It was quite inexplicable. My son saw an elderly gentleman walking down the stairs who then disappeared through a wall. The most strange thing I think were the boots seen walking through the restaurant, with no one in them! We got quite used to all this over the years.' Near the pub, Mr Stentson of Ollerton saw an apparition crossing the A614: 'I was cycling home one night when I saw this misty figure cross in front of me, going towards the abbey. I watched it reach the other side and then it simply faded away.'

In the abbey grounds the ghost of the Black Friar is said to have literally frightened a man to death at the turn of the century. The Black Friar is described as a tall figure wearing a black monk's cowl, with morbid, skeletal face beneath, the very image of 'Death' himself, minus his scythe. The Black Friar seems to be of identical appearance to the Newstead ghost of the same name. It is curious that there are three ghosts in the area with similar appearance, and the Cistercian monks at Rufford Abbey would have worn white habits not black. Do we have a travelling ghost in North Nottinghamshire, or is this an example of a recurring hallucination based on some fearful archetype from deep in the subconscious mind?

Apart from an obviously spectral appearance the White Lady, unlike the Black Friar, seems to be a benign lost soul and little has been heard of her of late. According to tradition, she would appear in the reflection of the mirror in the room that was once hers. The White Lady is said to be the ghost of Lady Arabella Stuart, whose unhappy life came to an early conclusion. Arabella was the issue of a secret marriage between Elizabeth Cavendish and Charles Lennox. Her parents both died prematurely, Charles in 1576, followed shortly by his wife. Arabella became the ward of her grandmother, Bess of Hardwick. Bess was truly a self-made woman whose ambition was boundless. Arabella was the nearest living relative to Elizabeth I and her royal blood made her a possible successor to the throne, but in an atmosphere of plots and intrigue she was seen as a threat to Elizabeth herself. Arabella was confined to Hardwick Hall, where her grandmother virtually kept her under house arrest. She found new freedom upon the accession to the throne of James I. Accepting James' patronage, Arabella became part of the royal court, but found herself increasingly frustrated by her dependence on the King's goodwill, her own income being very low. Her unsanctioned marriage to William Seymour once more involved her in political intrigue; like Elizabeth before him James now saw Arabella as a threat. She was confined to the Tower, where she died aged 30. It is said Arabella haunts Rufford because this is the only place in her short life where she was really happy.

A far more harrowing shade is that of a weeping child. Legend has it that in the past a child was chased through the abbey by an unknown assailant and, despite attempts to hide, was found and murdered. Guests of the Savilles staying at the abbey complained of restless nights, their sleep disturbed by mournful cries. Some had the unnerving experience of having the ghost of a cold, frightened child climb into their beds with them. No evidence of child murder at Rufford has come down to us, nor has any record of such a crime been found in the county's archives or court records. However, a house this old may have more than one 'skeleton in the cupboard'.

The old lady pushing a pram around the park could go unnoticed by those who met her, were it not for the obvious antiquity of her dress and the pram. This ghost seems to be a nanny, from perhaps the Victorian or Edwardian period. Those who have seen her have the impression that she is quite oblivious to them and is simply out walking the baby. There is also a tradition of a ghostly old lady appearing in St George's room in the abbey; whether this is the same ghost is unclear. Could these apparitions be more like 'time-slips' than a haunting?

The Stable Block Haunting

WITH dragons perched on the apex of the roof and cast iron gargoyles squatting on the conduits of the guttering, the stable block is the most complete set of buildings remaining from Rufford Abbey's halcyon days. The mellow red brick buildings form a square around a cobbled courtyard. In the early 1980s, the stable block was sympathetically refurbished to provide facilities for the increasing numbers of visitors coming to Rufford. A Craft Centre, with a shop and a gallery, was created, along with a book and gift shop across the courtyard. Above the craft shop, the Buttery Restaurant was built. When the courtyard cobbles were relaid bones were found beneath, presumably of monks lying in a long forgotten graveyard. There were also rumours that the builders had discovered more bodies inside the buildings, behind cupboards that had been fixed to walls for a time-out-of-memory. Many of the staff have had uncanny experiences here; it seems that echoes from Rufford's past still linger. Two of the longest serving staff are the catering supervisors, Susan Ilett and Margaret Morris. Margaret remembers several strange happenings that have occurred over the years.

'Where the information centre in the courtyard is now used to be a kiosk where we'd sell ice cream. I started working there when I first came. I worked on my own and soon noticed odd things happen. I would put things away at night, things like tea-towels, and know that I'd done it, but the next morning, when I opened up they'd moved. When I asked who'd been in there, no one had been. I had this gentleman come in the kiosk one day who said he was a medium and that he visited historic places across the country to get in touch with the vibrations. I took all this with a pinch of salt. While he was talking to me he said he had picked up a spirit. As I watched his face altered, his high cheek bones sank in and his voice changed. This really frightened me. He said there were several spirits about, but that they were all friendly and wouldn't do any harm. This really shook me.

We used to go for tea breaks in a little room, beyond an office that is now the book shop store room. On a particularly red-hot summer's day, I'd been really busy and the place was packed solid. Myself and one of the book shop staff, Anne Reeder, had our break together. We were both about done in. I fell into a chair and let out a deep sigh. From the room beyond the tea-room we heard the door open, a chair creak and someone else sigh loudly as they sat down. We both laughed at this and I said, "Someone else had a hard day! I'll go and see if they want a cup of tea." When I looked there was no one there. Yet both Anne and I heard someone quite clearly. It was funny for a moment, until we thought about it.

'In the Craft Centre there have been a couple of weird things happen too. It feels different in there. I don't like being left on my own there after late night functions. In the Buttery there are some swing doors into the servery. As I watched them they swung open, as if someone had walked through. There was no blast of wind or anything else to account for this.'

Susan Ilett has also had odd experiences in the Buttery: 'I've been here about fifteen years and in those days we didn't have the Coach House as a restaurant, only the Buttery. I was working there on my own, cleaning the floor by the counter area. Well, I'm on my knees scrubbing away when the cutlery starts rattling in the trays. I looked up to see why. I was at eye level with it, and the cutlery raised up. Not all of it, just the odd fork. It didn't lift out of the tray, just stood up on end. I was stunned.

'One Saturday morning I was in the back of the servery area in the Buttery, when I heard the door at the far end of the restaurant open. I heard someone walking through and thought from the sound of the footsteps going up the steps at the far end that it was Steve, one of the staff. The door opened, and this person went out. I followed, looking for Steve to see why he hadn't spoken to me, but he wasn't there. I must have been disturbed about this because another member of staff, Caroline, came in and said "Whatever is the matter Sue, you look like you've seen a ghost!" I told her what had happened and as we were talking the same thing happened again while she was there.'

The Buttery is on the second floor above the craft shop. At the top of the stairs leading into the Buttery is a door marked 'Staff Only'. Behind the door is long corridor, with leaded windows looking down onto the courtyard and rooms leading off that were once the servants' lodgings. The 1861 census return for Rufford Abbey provides us with a snapshot of life in the 'Rooms above the Stables'. In room 9 lived Robert Allen, Second Whip of Hounds. In rooms 10, 11, 12 lived the stable hands, Henry King, John

Steadman and Joseph Page. In room 13 was John Ward, the groom, his wife Harriet and their two daughters, Ann and Emma, both dressmakers. In room 14 lived Joseph Watkinson, 'General Servant in the Stables', his wife Ellen, their two sons, Joseph aged 9 and Tom 1, and two daughters, Francis 11 and Elizabeth aged 7.

The prep kitchen used by the catering staff today was originally the kitchen used by the servants lodging in the stable block. Susan Ilett has had several strange experiences in this part of the building: 'Along the corridor to the prep kitchen you can often feel a presence, as if someone is there. The prep kitchen has definitely got a cold feeling about it, even in midsummer. Many of the staff here have noticed it. For a while the kitchen was used as a staff room. Apparently, several people when coming in there for a break would just briefly see someone sitting in a tin bath in front of the fireplace – which is now blocked off – this would fade away as they watched.

'One time we'd had a very late night, and I was alone in the prep kitchen clearing up. The door to the Buttery was ajar and I could hear what I took to be Catharine – one of the staff – calling me as she approached the kitchen along the corridor. She was a long time arriving and she was still talking to me. I couldn't make out what she was saying, and called back "What's that you say, I can't hear you?" I got so rattled that in the end I went to see what she wanted. There was no one in the corridor at all. I went to the doorway of the Buttery and looked across to the far side of the restaurant, and I could see Catharine working on the dishwasher in the servery. This was immediately after I'd heard this voice. Later I asked what she wanted. She said she hadn't called me or been down the corridor where the prep kitchen was.

'On another occasion I thought someone had gone by the kitchen door so I went to the door to see who it was. As I looked to the right, just before the fire doors, in the arch set in the wall, I glimpsed this floating, foggy, smoke-like form. It had its back to me. I could make out that its hair was mousy coloured, smooth on top, and ending in long, curly tendrils, a bit like the dreadlocks they have today. I didn't see the face. Then it was gone.'

Margaret Morris concludes: 'When I first came here in 1981 there were reports of people seeing a woman and child looking out of the upper windows of the stable block when it was known that there was no one in there. This caused some anxiety with the staff. I was telling my mum about this and she told me of a local lady called Mrs Starbrook who had been a laundry maid here and lived in the quarters above the stable. She had been so frightened by what used to happen there that she was moved elsewhere on the estate and went to stay in West Lodge. Mrs Starbrook had told my mum this before I mentioned any of it. So, this seems to be independent confirmation that you can't simply brush off.'

SHERWOOD FOREST

Sacred Trees and Magic Woods

IN his *History of Nottinghamshire*, Robert Thorton captures the romance of Sherwood Forest: 'We are now arrived at that portion of our history where we must tread (I had almost said classic) magic ground, where beings like fairies danced, where deer sported in groups unnumbered, and in limit almost unbounded; where Robin Hood, and his gay followers, performed their many and renowned exploits.'

The name Sherwood has been taken to mean the 'shire wood' – the forest once covered most of Nottinghamshire. It probably became a Royal Forest soon after the Norman Conquest, one of the 90 or so Royal Forests that were the private hunting grounds of the monarch.

Sherwood Forest is 'Robin Hood Country'. Old maps in the county's libraries and archives show many places and natural features named after the outlaw hero. Near Papplewick is a cave known as 'Robin Hood's Stable' and not far off are 'Robin Hood's Hills', in Kirkby Forest. Here was once 'Robin Hood's Chair', a seat cut into the rock above a panoramic view. According to William Harrod, writing in 1801, this was destroyed in about 1780, the rock of 'Robin Hood's Chair' being cut up for use in landscaping the lake at Newstead Abbey. On the far side of Kirkby Forest, on the other side of the railway line, is another 'Robin Hood's Cave'. In the 1871 census for Blidworth the recorder, Mr Clarke, wrote notes in longhand concerning the 'Robin Hood's Cave' that once stood on the south side of Cave Pond, otherwise known as Cave Dam. Mr Clarke relates that his father remembered the cave's destruction in about 1750. According to the historian Joseph Whittaker, the cave was cut into a sandstone outcrop that jutted out into the waters. Place-names are not hard evidence for Robin Hood's actual existence, yet they do show us how deeply the legends became embedded into the imagination of the local people and so became, quite literally, part of the landscape.

Sherwood Forest Country Park has some of the finest ancient oak woodlands in western Europe. The famous 'Major Oak', often thought of as the meeting place of Robin Hood and his outlaws, was named after Major Hayman Rooke of Woodhouse Place, a local antiquarian who first described it in a book in 1799. Before 1800 it had been called the Queen's Oak. The tree became known locally as the 'Major's Oak' and this was later simplified to the 'Major Oak'. Though its huge girth of 32 ft 10 inches proclaims its antiquity – the Major Oak is thought to be about 600 years old – it wouldn't even have been an acorn in Robin's day. Rivalling the Major Oak was 'Robin Hood's Larder', once a mighty tree with a hollow centre. Vandals are suspected of setting fire to this tree, whose burnt out shell was blown down in a gale in 1961. Similarly, the 'Simon Forest Oak', described at the turn of the century as an enormous, thriving tree, was all but destroyed by fire. King John and Edward I are both said to have held court beneath 'Parliament Oak' whilst hunting in the Royal Forest. Now a decayed, ruinous sight, it only survives at all by being chained to a younger tree. Perhaps the mightiest and oldest of them all was the 'Greendale Oak'. This majestic tree had an arch cut through it by Duke of Portland in 1724, a wanton act which was done for a bet with the 2nd Earl of Oxford, so that the Duke could drive his carriage through it. Our pagan ancestors held trees as sacred, magic entities. The 'temples' of the Celts were the 'nemeton', sacred groves, usually of oaks, where sacrifices both human and animal were offered to the gods. Sherwood would certainly have had such 'holy places'. In northern Europe the oak was the sacred tree of the god Bel. Sir James Frazer in his seminal work *The Golden Bough* has shown that the oak in particular was sacred to many Indo-European peoples. It is still a potent symbol used by a variety of businesses and agencies, the National Trust for example.

Robin of Sherwood – A Real Man?

THE question 'Who was Robin Hood?' has never been satisfactorily answered. In *W'dhus and the Wolfhunters*, David Bradbury points out that, because many Sherwood Forest records have survived 'from the 1260s onwards, we know the names of virtually everyone who was ever found guilty of cutting tree branches, or suspected of poaching', but the name of Robin Hood is conspicuously absent. However, Mr Bradbury points out that there was a 'Robert Hood' of Yorkshire, who fled the law in 1225 and rapidly acquired himself the nickname 'Hobbehod' (possibly by association with the elusive sprite of folklore 'Hodthurst', known to southerners as 'Robin Goodfellow'), whose exploits may have inspired some of the early Robin Hood ballads, which are set in Yorkshire. Despite the hundreds of hours of painstaking work by historians no documentary evidence for the existence of Robin Hood of Sherwood Forest has been found.

The earliest surviving reference to Robin Hood appears in the poem by William Langland, *Piers the Plowman*, circa 1377. A more developed version appears around 1500 in the *Lyttle Geste of Robyne Hode*. Neither King Richard I or the Sheriff of Nottingham appear in these early sources. The *Lyttle Geste* places Robin in the reign of King Henry III (1216–72), who succeeded his brother John 17 years after Richard's death in 1199. There was no Sheriff of

Nottingham until 1499. Little John appears early in the *Geste*, but Maid Marian and Friar Tuck do not. The first mention we have of Maid Marian comes from a poem by a 14th-century French monk. The poem has her as a shepherdess and Robin as a shepherd. There was an important Benedictine monastery at Blyth, built in 1088 by the Norman knight Roger de Busli. The house belonged to St Katerine's Priory in Rouen and was manned chiefly by Norman monks. Friar Tuck it seems would not have been out of place there. Dom David Knowles in *The Religious Orders in England* describes how in 1287 a 'criminous monk' from Blyth was sent back to Rouen, followed by another 'undesirable' the following year. Blyth was on the northern fringe of Sherwood in Robin's time. It lay on the old Great North Road, the main road between London and York, and on the route of Stone Street, the ancient trackway running to Nottingham. It was also on the main route between Sherwood and Barnsdale, Robin's other famous forest haunt. Blyth appears as a place-name in many Robin Hood stories, ancient and modern.

Woden, the Green Man and Robin Hood

IF the Robin Hood legends do not describe actual events, from where do these stories come? After looking at all the evidence, Mr W. H. Stevenson in *Notes about Notts* (published in 1874) concludes: 'In the face of such a combined array of facts, as they advance, I think we are bound to accept the existence of Robin Hood as a medieval myth, sprung from the mists of Teutonic Paganism, garnished by the prolific muses of the English minstrels, that survived the wreck of time, and which will live as long as the English language.' According to tradition, Robin fought for the natural rights of the native English population, Anglo-Saxons, with perhaps some Celtic blood in their veins. The invading Normans had overturned their world, stolen their lands, usurped their laws and institutions and all but enslaved them. However, the Anglo-Saxons (the 'Teutonic Pagans' that Stevenson refers to) had been invaders themselves. From the 5th century onwards they fought the incumbent Celts for the land, bringing with them their own pantheon of gods. Might not the native population have drawn on the imagery of the gods of their forefathers to create a new hero for themselves in their time of oppression under the Normans?

Robin dressed in 'Lincoln Green' shares imagery with that of the Celtic Green Man, who appears in churches and cathedrals throughout Europe as 'foliate head' carvings in stone and wood. Usually he is depicted as just a head with foliage coming out of his mouth and sometimes ears. The medieval masons who carved him sought to invoke a powerful 'spirit', what we would term an archetype, whose origins were pre-Christian. Southwell Minster in Nottinghamshire, on the eastern fringes of Sherwood Forest, has some of the finest foliage carvings in Europe, known as the 'Leaves of Southwell Minster'. These carvings are densely populated with foliate heads. The Green Man is essentially the embodiment of the irresistible dynamic of the circle of life and death and rebirth, mirroring the cycle of the seasons; it is this concept that the masons sought to express. The Green Man is also the Jack-in-the-Green from folk songs and nursery rhymes and is recalled as the name of countless pubs across Britain. Both the Green Man and Robin Hood are still invoked in folk customs across the British Isles, especially those connected with May Day. In pre-Christian Europe 'Beltane', the festival that marked the end of winter and the coming of new life with spring, was in May. Surviving as May Day, these festivities had long been viewed suspiciously by religious zealots like the Elizabethan Puritan Philip Stubbes: '. . . this May Pole (this stinking Idol rather) which is covered all over with flours and herbs bound about with strings . . . And thus being is reared up, with handkerchiefs and flags hovering over the top . . . and then fall they to dance about it like heathen peoples did at the dedication of Idols'.

May Day celebrations were often called 'the Robin Hood Games'. In the heart of 'Robin Hood Country', the village of Wellow boasts one of the tallest maypoles in England. It stands on the village green all the year round. Not far off, in Edwinstowe, is St Mary's church, where by tradition Robin and Maid Marian were married. Whilst there is no documentary evidence for this happy event, Edwinstowe would have been the ideal location. Set in the heart of Sherwood Forest, it would have provided easy access and swift egress for the outlaws back into the forest. The village grew up around the chapel of St Edwin, for it was here that the body of King Edwin of Northumbria was brought after the battle of Hatfield Chase in AD 632. Edwin fought against the combined forces of Penda and Cadwallon, both pagans. For this he was martyred and Edwinstowe became a site for pilgrimage.

The Protestant Reformation produced a violent reaction against May Day celebrations. In 1644 Parliament banned maypoles altogether as a 'heathenish vanity' and throughout the Commonwealth period 'Maying' was strongly discouraged on the grounds that 'of fortie, three score or a hundred maides going into the wood overnight there have scaresly the third part of them returned home again undefiled'. The 19th-century revival of Maying saw it sanitised to suit Victorian tastes. With the more obvious fertility aspects removed May Day became 'a pretty thing for children'.

However, it would be a mistake to attempt to supersede the need for an historical Robin by simply identifying him with a single ancient deity or hero figure, whatever striking parallels there may be.

SHIREOAKS

The Devil's Wood and Sir Thomas Hewitt

Your hooves have stamped at the black margin of the wood

(W. B. Yeats, *On a Picture of a Black Centaur by Edmund Dulac*)

THE village of Shireoaks, west of Worksop, although not mentioned in the Domesday Book, has been a settlement since Saxon times. On the estate of Shireoaks Hall is Scratta Wood. In his book *Whitwell and Barlborough*, Capt Roy Peters writes that: 'The Anglo-Saxon scraette means "harlot", an unlikely name for a wood, although the imaginative reader could devise a reason for such a name. Much more likely is the Anglo-Saxon scratta or scritta which means "devil". There is a similar Viking word skratti, which means "goblin", "monster", or "devil". Obviously therefore we have the sense of a wood in which some kind of devil or monster was suppose to reside.' We do not know what ancient horror gave the wood its name, but Scratta Wood has always been a place of mystery. Deep within it are Iron Age burial mounds. Regarding them, one elderly local resident was heard to say, 'There are three devil rings in Scratta Wood.' Few people venture near the wood after dark. For many years there have been stories of unearthly blue lights seen glowing amidst the trees at night. Described by one witness as 'like a ball of blue fire', the lights have been seen to shadow passers-by, but never to leave the wood.

During the reign of Charles II, Thomas Hewitt inherited Shireoaks Hall on the death of his father. Sir Thomas was born at the hall on 9th September 1656 and educated at the famous public school at Shrewsbury and at Christchurch College, Oxford. On inheriting the estate, he became an officer of King Charles' Yeomanry Guard. These were hedonistic times. Sir Thomas earned himself the reputation of a rake, even at the licentious court of King Charles. He was an outspoken atheist and baited Christians at every opportunity, but his unorthodox beliefs did him no permanent harm at court, it seems. He later served as Surveyor General of the Woods to William III and then to George I. Sir Thomas had wealth and privilege enough to indulge in any vice that took his fancy and his debauchery scandalised the countryside. His first act as master of Shireoaks Hall was to give his ancestral home a new entrance hall. He then laid out an avenue, graced by an elaborate arch, linking this new entrance to the haunted wood. Thomas then built a pagan temple in the wood, its eerie reputation appealing to his macabre sense of humour. No expense was spared in its construction for it was to serve ultimately as Sir Thomas' final resting place, his own mausoleum. When it was completed, the temple was two storeys high and decorated in sumptuous style, with murals and statues. It is said that the two reception rooms downstairs were decorated entirely as representations of Sir Thomas' own visions of heaven and hell. What uses the upstairs rooms were put to is not recorded. The wood, being some distance from the hall itself, allowed Sir Thomas and his band of pleasure-crazed bacchanals to make merry in the temple undisturbed. Wild feasts continued sometimes for days on end until all attending were either satiated or exhausted. Sir Thomas' licentious appetites, however, are said to have surpassed them all.

Sir Thomas had one child, a daughter, named Mary. Apparently, she had inherited all her mother's strength of character and all her father's eccentricity. There was a gypsy encampment near Shireoaks Hall at a place called Gateford, a place-name that is still in use. Mary and some friends went there to visit a fortune teller called Thackeray. Once alone in his tent with her, Thackeray was able to convince her that, by the aid of a magic mirror, he could reveal the face of the man she would marry. She looked into the mirror and saw Thackeray's own face gazing back at her. Whether by magic or trickery, she was beguiled. Mary ran away with Thackeray, the gypsy, and married him. Sir Thomas was furious. He disowned his daughter and forbade anyone to mention her name again.

The sad fate of Sir Thomas' only child isn't known for sure. One tradition has it that Thackeray abandoned his now penniless wife, though not before she gave him children. Years later some gypsies claiming to be the descendants of Thackeray and Mary pursued an unsuccessful claim on the Hewitt estates through the courts. There is a story that she returned to her family home in a wretched state. On her father's orders she was turned from the door and she is said to have perished either by her own hand or to have died from a broken heart. Another darker tale has it that Thackeray was the Devil himself come to enact dreadful punishment on Sir Thomas for his godlessness, by stealing his daughter from him. Whatever Thackeray's motives were, the loss of his daughter did nothing to impede Sir Thomas' atheism or his carnality.

Seeking a new heir for his estate, Sir Thomas sent for his nephew John Hewitt, the rector of Harthill. Sir Thomas promised to leave him all his fortune if he would give up his ministry. John refused temptation and replied, 'No! What account should I give my God if I forsake these, the souls committed to my charge?' Sir Thomas is said to have laughed at this show of piety, 'Thou fearst God! I fear neither God nor devil. If there be a devil let him fly away with my soul.' And so it seems Sir Thomas damned himself.

His godson, Sir Thomas Thornborough of Osberton, became heir, but there was a codicil to the will that on Thornborough's death the estate would revert to a Hewitt, namely Sir Thomas' great-nephew John. In due course this codicil was enacted, but with a consequence that ultimately frustrated Sir Thomas' purpose for, as the Reverend John Hewitt, his great-nephew used his godless uncle's wealth for all manner of good works. Sir Thomas died soon after his will was amended. Possibly with some warning of his impending death, he had hastened the work on his mausoleum, declaring that this and not the hallowed ground of a churchyard was to be his final resting place. His family were appalled. They let it be known that, whatever the old man had said, Sir Thomas would be given Christian burial with his forebears in the churchyard at the nearby village of Wales.

However, Sir Thomas' friends and loyal servants sought to carry out the old man's wishes. They removed his body, then filled the coffin with stones and sealed it. Then at midnight in a torchlight procession they bore the corpse to the mausoleum. As the cortège rounded the fringe of Scratta Wood a great wind blew up and extinguished all the torches. They stood in trepidation, fearing the wind as some ill omen. Suddenly a figure leapt at the mourners from out of the wood. Terrified, they dropped the corpse and fled. When they had regained their courage and returned the body was gone. The official version has it that the family recovered the body and it lies in Wales churchyard to this day. However, legend relates that it was 'Old Scratch', the Devil himself, that leapt from the wood, and claimed Sir Thomas Hewitt, body and soul.

SKEGBY

The Skegby Hall Ghosts

LIKE so many old mansions Skegby Hall, near Sutton-in-Ashfield, has been altered and put to different uses by each succeeding generation. At one time it was an Approved School – but the headmasters there had more than the educational needs of the community's most challenging pupils to contend with. The headmaster's residential accommodation, in a part of the hall dating back to around 1720, was haunted. The ghost was said to be seen by successive headmasters over many years. The older part of the building, reputedly dating back to the 14th century, is haunted by a ghostly funeral cortège, the cowled figures of monks, bearing a coffin and singing a dirge, drifting through the rooms. The building is no longer used as a school and now serves as offices for the Social Services Department of the County Council. According to the District Manager, Mr Stephen Roe, none of the present staff at Skegby Hall have reported experiencing anything paranormal so far.

SOUTHWELL

The Ghosts of the Saracen's Head

THE Saracen's Head is a hotel in the centre of historic Southwell. The earliest record of buildings on this site is from 1396 and part of the present building could well date back that far. During alterations in 1986 painted wall decorations were found that date from the 1500s. More wall paintings have been found since, one showing foliage and fruit, another with part of the Arthurian story of Sir Galahad in verse, in a border below the ceiling. King Charles I spent his last night of freedom here in 1646. The old inn is a piece of living history, with more than its share of romance and ghosts.

The ghost that has appeared to Cathy, one of the waitresses, was seen, 'through a glass, darkly . . .' Whilst preparing the tables in the restaurant she has noticed, reflected in the picture-glass of the paintings adorning the walls, a young girl moving behind her. When she has turned to look, 'face to face', Cathy has found herself quite alone in the room. From brief glimpses of the shade Cathy describes the girl as of small build, wearing 19th-century-style dress. In the laundry room upstairs Cathy has also been made to feel uneasy by a presence that chills the air. Despite the absence of any visible manifestation, Cathy feels that the presence is Lord Byron, who lived in Southwell for a while and stayed at the Saracen's Head. During his lifetime Byron caused the maids in inns and hotels across Europe to feel uneasy; but his motives were decidedly earthly rather than ethereal. This ominous atmosphere has also been felt by the housekeeper, Annie, who has worked at the hotel for a number of years: 'There is a weird, cold feeling in there. I can be in there hours sorting things out, with no problem. Then you suddenly get this chill. On the corridor there is a certain door marked "No Entry". There is a sensation that there is someone behind that door, almost if they're about to put their hand around the door. I've also had the awful feeling of something dangling across my face, like a spider's web there. I looked but there was nothing there. I've often run to the laundry room and run back. That part of the hotel really does frighten me.' On the same landing as the laundry cupboard is another store room where one of the staff saw a ghost in a suit of armour floating above the floor.

The main focus of hauntings at the Saracen's Head seems to be bedroom number 1, King Charles' Room. Annie recalls that some guests have spent restless nights in this room: 'In room 1 there is a blast of cold air that wakes people up. We had a gentleman from the Spiritualist church stay there once and he was quite petrified by the feeling in that room. Several guests have mentioned this icy blast. Outside this room guests have heard people walking about at night, but when they've looked out no one is there. This happens down the main staircase too. The receptionists have heard people coming down but when they have looked up from the desk to serve them, there's no one.'

King Charles arrived at the inn on the morning of 5th May 1646, disguised as a clergyman. Exhausted, he collapsed on the bed in the room occupied by his emissary Jean de Montreuil, who was at Southwell to negotiate secretly with the Scottish forces besieging Newark. Lord Lothian, the Scottish Commissioner, wrote to the English forces falsely claiming Charles had arrived unexpectedly at Southwell and later handed him over to Parliamentary forces, sealing the King's fate. Charles was beheaded in 1649. As a matter of political expediency the inn changed its name from the King's Arms to the Saracen's Head. Oliver Cromwell is said to have used the same room as the King when he stayed at Southwell in 1648.

Ian, one of the waiters, had his own weird experiences at the hotel: 'Sometimes we staff have to stay overnight here. One night I was lying in bed and l could hear people walking about outside the room. This is at about 1.30 am. So I jumped up like a shot and looked outside the room, but there was nobody there. Then one Friday night there were about five of us in the bar, at about half two in the morning, when suddenly we could hear these people talking and walking about upstairs. This went on for about five or ten minutes. We sat on the stairs and listened to them. The sounds were coming from the front of the building. So then we shot upstairs, but there was no one there. When I first came here . . . there was a receptionist here; she slept in the King's room and saw two blue lights come out of the wall. She didn't sleep in there again. I know that the night porter has heard things, the floorboards on the stair creaking like people walking about. One night a lady, in some distress, ran down to tell him that there was an old man in her room. When he went up to look there was no one there.'

Whilst visiting the hotel in the course of my research, I met Mr and Mrs Bellamy. They have stayed at the hotel, and often stop in for coffee if they are in Southwell. 'We were staying here, with our son and daughter, Sarah, in the new part of the hotel, in the stable yard. We stayed for several weeks. One night, I was putting them to bed, and Sarah asked me not to put the light off. She said that there had been two faces looking down at her as she lay in bed. She described them quite thoroughly. She must have been about seven or eight, at that age she wouldn't have been able to make this up. From that day on she couldn't sleep with the light off, it must have cost us a fortune over the years.'

This is not the only time that the family have experienced the uncanny. 'During the 1980s we lived in the village of Elksley, in a huge Georgian house called Portland Farm. My middle daughter, Caroline, saw something there. She refused to sleep in this one bedroom, she used to sleep on the landing. She would say to me, "Mummy whenever I try to go to sleep there's a lady at the side of the bed." I said to her, just turn over and go to sleep, "I do," she said, "but she keeps walking round to the other side." I heard things there, but didn't want to frighten the children, so didn't say much about it. On one occasion when I was alone in the house I heard this terrible coughing coming from upstairs. I thought it was the dog, but when I looked the dog was asleep in the utility room. In this same bedroom I also saw the rocking chair, moving on its own, then stop abruptly. I never felt frightened there, but I felt there was someone watching me.'

Musical Ghosts at the Bramley Apple

THE Bramley Apple in Southwell is on the old coaching road to Newark. Originally called the George and Dragon, the pub was renamed after a brief period of closure in the 1970s. Southwell is the home of the Bramley apple, first cultivated by the Brailsford sisters in their father's cottage garden in the early 1800s and 'discovered' in about 1856 by local nurseryman Henry Merryweather when a Mr Bramley owned the cottage.

For over 50 years the pub was run by the Johnson-Copper family. Sarah Johnson-Copper and her husband took over the pub just after World War I. When the present landlord George Reynolds and his wife Dorothy experienced some uncanny happenings at the pub it was to one of their regulars, Vincent Johnson-Copper, grandson of

Sarah, that they turned for answers. George had experienced unexplained mischief in the cellar. He told me that to draw real ale from the wood the barrel must first be tapped and a wooden peg or bung inserted as the beer settles. Once it is ready this peg is removed and is always carefully left on top of the barrel for future use. If the peg isn't taken out a vacuum is formed as the ale is pumped through, so little beer will reach the pump. Several times, especially on busy evenings, the beer has suddenly stopped flowing. Suspecting an empty barrel, George has been dismayed to find the wooden peg inserted firmly in the barrel, cutting off the beer. George is emphatic that this could only be done deliberately; the peg could not possibly get in the barrel by itself. Vincent spent much of his boyhood at the pub, and later served as relief manager there on several occasions. He did indeed throw some light on the Reynolds' experiences and had some of his own to add: 'I would suggest that it is the biggest, certainly the lowest, cellar in Southwell. There are 13 steps down. My grandmother was teetotal, never had a drink of beer in her life. When she sent grandfather down there for a jug of ale he had to whistle all the way there and all the way back, so she'd know if he'd stopped to take a drink! It was a family tradition to be very particular about the cellar, it was always kept spotless. The walls were whitewashed once a month and fresh papers, to catch any spillage, were put down on the floor every day. I've often had this feeling down there of being watched, almost as if something would happen if I didn't do things just right. On this particular night I had gone into the cellar to put another barrel on. I pulled the peg out, turned the tap on, went upstairs and started to pull the beer through. It was sucking back on me, it wouldn't let me pull it. I went back down into the cellar again and the peg had been put back in and the tap turned off. I knew that I'd just done it. I've known the gas for the keg beers go off, when you know you've switched it on.'

There were other reminders of the Johnson-Coppers' long association with the pub: 'Michael, George's son, asked me if there had been any musical connection with the pub. I told him that my uncle, Eric Ross, had been organist at the Minster and that there used to be several pianos about the place. My father and his sister were also musical; Father played the violin and his sister the piano. This fair near knocked his duck off! He has heard music in the pub at night coming from some unknown source.'

Upstairs are the landlord's private quarters and some residential accommodation. Along the stairs and corridor have been heard the tramping feet of some invisible visitors. Michael in particular has experienced the sounds of someone approaching his room and has seen the door suddenly open, only to show the empty corridor beyond and himself totally alone upstairs.

Whilst acting as caretaker manager Vincent experienced a more tangible display of unseen forces at the pub: 'My wife, myself and some friends were having a late night drink in the bar. After everyone had gone we cleared up and left some clean glasses on the bar towels at the end of the counter. We were lying in bed when I heard something moving below in the pub. I could hear someone going into the cellar and bring bottles up. I could the bottles rattling in the crates. I went downstairs and from the door leading into the bar could see all the glasses that had been on the counter were smashed on the floor. There was no one about, no cat or anything like that in the place. I shot straight back upstairs, didn't even sweep the glass up until the morning. In the morning I could see that things had been moved all over the place. The front part of the pub used to be the living room for the family years ago. This is where they found my Uncle Eric dead, with his head in the fire grate. He'd gone down for some peppermint, he'd had indigestion after a Rotary dinner, collapsed and died. It was almost as if someone didn't approve of our after-hours session the previous night.'

Ballroom Charlie

THE Admiral Rodney in Southwell is a Grade II listed building and was once a coaching inn. The pub has been haunted for many years by the ghost of a bearded man, nicknamed Charlie by the regulars. Mr and Mrs Selby kept the pub for over nine years and though told of its reputation they were at first sceptical about the ghost. However, their experiences and those of their son Nick made them think again.

Behind the pub itself is an old ballroom, beyond a half-glass door on a landing reached via a short flight of stairs. It is through this glass door that the spectral form of the bearded man stares out. Now sadly neglected, the ballroom has been put to many uses over the years. The Rodney School at Kirklington began there as a school of dance and drama and took its name from the pub. During the war soldiers from a searchlight outfit were billeted in the ballroom. Could the ghost be connected in some way to one of the alternative uses that the room has been put to?

In all the bearded man was seen three times by members of the Selby family. Mrs Marcia Selby remembers her encounter with him well: 'I only saw him the once and that was enough. I didn't want to see him again. I was taking the tills up to the office to lock them away. I don't know why but I glanced at the ballroom door and I saw this face staring at me through the glass. It was a man staring at me from inside the ballroom. I could see him quite distinctly. He had dark hair and beard. He was just staring. It really frightened me and I ran down those stairs pretty quick. There is no way this was a reflection or anything like that.'

Nick Selby has never forgotten his encounters with Charlie: 'There was always an atmosphere on that landing, you couldn't explain it. I was about 14 when I first saw it. I came up the stairs and saw this bearded man looking out through the glass door of the ballroom at me. It really frightened me. I went racing downstairs to tell Dad that there was someone in the ballroom. He had a look but there was no one there. I saw him again and I never liked to stay long on the landing after that.'

Mr Selby recalls other odd occurrences connected with the ballroom: 'At one time a number of lads used it for weight training. It was an unused room and they used it as their gym two or three times a week. They always kept the door open. They always used to say it was spooky up there. Our dog would never stay in there either. One of our cooks had a friend who was a medium and she came to look at the room. She didn't stay long. She said there were cold spots in the room. I jokingly said that there was a draught coming from somewhere, but she was most insistent. She said there was a definite presence in the room and she could feel vibrations. I said it was the disco downstairs, trying to make light of it. She got quite angry about it. She was sure something was wrong with that room. She said she'd like to come back again but she never did. Whenever there were funny noises about the pub late at night we always used to say, "It's all right, it's only Charlie." '

Following my interview with the Selbys, I wrote to the present manager, Mr Alan Boultby, to inquire whether Charlie still haunted the Admiral Rodney. He wrote back as follows: 'Your information is correct with regard to the Rodney and a supposed ghost. The owner Mr Joe Chiarella has witnessed several happenings. Whilst I have not seen anything to confirm the fact there are several people who have witnessed strange happenings. These include a piano playing by itself, lights being switched on and off, cellar equipment acting in a strange manner and many other things.'

A new feature of the Admiral Rodney is Charlie's Bar. Whether it was named after the resident ghost or not, those sampling the excellent beverages available there should be aware that they may well be in the presence of spirits other than the bottled variety.

THORNEY

A Murderer's Ghost

THE village of Thorney, in the district of Newark and Sherwood, is typical of the scattered farming communities of north Nottinghamshire. Here, however, the ghost of

Tom Otter is said to wander the lanes. Tom was a notorious highwayman who terrorised travellers on the Great North Road and he was thought to have had a hideout in a cave under Muskham bridge. In March 1806 Tom was hanged for murdering his wife on their wedding night. His body was left to rot on the gibbet at Byards Leap, near Leadenham, a place famous in folklore for the prodigious jump made by a horse frightened by a witch.

THURGARTON

The Black Canon

THE name of this village is Norse for 'the farm of Thorgeirr'. A ghost of a Black Canon is said to walk abroad here. In medieval times Thurgarton was a minor ecclesiastical centre, with a church and an Augustinian priory founded in 1187. The Augustinians were known as the White Friars despite wearing black habits, and should not be confused with the Black Friars who were the Dominicans. Thurgarton's Black Canon is more the archetypal figure of Death, a hooded phantom very much like the Black Monk at Newstead and Rufford. The village church is all that remains of the priory and has suffered from Victorian restoration; Pevsner describes it as 'a terribly mangled fragment'. The priory itself survived until 1777, when John Gilbert Cooper demolished the southwest tower and the bulk of the buildings to make way for a brick house, which became the Bishop of Southwell's residence between 1884 and 1909.

TUXFORD

Hell on Earth

TUXFORD is a sleepy little market town, just off the A1 between Newark and Retford. A place less like the infernal regions as described by Dante it is hard to imagine. However, Mr Robert Stretton Wilson of Tuxford Hall sought to create 'Hell on Earth' in this quiet backwater. From *White's Directory* we can see that Robert had risen from a maltster on Lincoln Street, Tuxford, in 1879, to Mr Wilson MRCVS, veterinary surgeon, by 1881. Described by contemporary sources as a wealthy eccentric, Mr Wilson acquired Tuxford Hall (built circa 1785) in about 1880. He set to work laying out one corner of the grounds to represent his own vision of the 'Devil's Garden'. Entering through a roughly hewn stone archway, visitors were met by a statue of Satan himself; Old Nick was crouching on top of a pillar, heavily wrapped in chains, with a skull in his hands. Beyond this was the 'Pit of Damnation', peopled by more statues of souls in torment. Amongst those Mr Wilson saw as deserving of this fate were 'The Chattering Charwoman', 'The Person with the Hard Heart' and, for reasons best known to himself, 'The President of the Primrose League'. Hell in Tuxford has long since gone though the hall itself remains, but if Mr Wilson's creation had been saved it would have doubtless proved a major tourist attraction. There was also a 'Devil's Garden' at Normanton on Soar and the 'Devil's Elbow' at Sutton Bonington. Unlike Mr Wilson's Hell, however, these were not man-made. It is likely that they were areas of wild uncultivated land that local folklore deemed an appropriate habitat for Beelzebub and his creatures.

WARSOP

'Warsop: where they leave their doors open'

AN unexpected light is thrown on the Robin Hood connection with Warsop by *The Oxford Book of English Place-names*. It gives the early spellings for Warsop as Waresope, Wareshope, Warsopa in 1180, Waresop and Warshop in 1233, and suggests that the 'hop' element of the name means 'valley' in Old English, the ending of Worksop having the same meaning. The first part of the name 'Warsop' could be a personal name such as waer, meaning 'cautious', or it could be from 'wearg', Old English for 'outlaw'. So, according to this source, Warsop could mean either 'the cautious valley', somewhere to be on your guard, or 'the outlaw's valley'. Even today the folk-memory of Warsop's outlaw past survives. This place-name evidence predates considerably the time of Robin Hood, the 12th century, and shows that the area had long been the haunt of outlaws, a kind of 'Dark Age Wild West', a no-man's land. Robin Hood was part of a long line of renegades seeking sanctuary from the law in this part of Sherwood Forest. The local saying 'Warsop: where they leave their doors open' refers not to a crime-free 'good-old-days' but to the time when each house in the village provided a ready bolt-hole for fugitives from the law.

The Vicar's Yarns

THE Rev James (Jim) Rooke grew up in Warsop. A retired teacher, he was ordained late in life and now has his own parish in the Lake District. All who meet this generous man, not unlike a clerical Mr Pickwick, are beguiled by his dry wit and down-to-earth demeanour. As a boy he was told of local legends and superstitions, and once saw a ghost himself. Jim's father was the captain of the bell-ringers. The family had always been strong churchgoers and Warsop church was something of a second home to

Jim. With other lads of the village he would often play amongst the gravestones whilst waiting for choir practice to start. The boys used to enjoy frightening each other with a superstition that you could see the devil by running around the church twelve times, within the chimes of midnight, holding your nose, and looking through the keyhole – variations of this superstition are found all over the country. Whilst playing in the churchyard one winter's evening, Jim noticed that a light was showing in the windows of the old rectory. He stopped to look and it seemed as if someone was carrying a lamp between the rooms. The rector, the Rev Cornwall, did not approve of youngsters playing in the churchyard, so Jim kept a lookout for his approach. The boys continued their game as the twilight dimmed to dusk, then Jim saw the figure of the rector, his dog-collar white in the gloom, walking along the path from the rectory to the church. The boys scattered.

Arriving home breathless from running, he mentioned to his father that he'd seen the rector going towards the church. His father was surprised at this, 'You can't have Jim, the rector's on holiday.' Jim was most insistent and told his father about the lights he'd seen moving about the rectory. Mr Rooke, accepting the boy's word, became concerned. Was someone robbing the rectory? Jim's insistence prompted Mr Rooke to fetch a constable. The grounds of the rectory were searched, but no intruders were found, so the rector was called back from his holiday to open the house. Inside, nothing had been taken and there were no signs of forced entry. Although Rev Cornwall was put out at having to cut short his holiday, Jim was not punished for wasting everyone's time – this was not the first time that strange things had been seen in the rectory.

On one occasion Christopher, the rector's son, was ill with a fever. When his mother took him up some food he asked her, 'What did the doctor say, mum?' His mother was puzzled as no doctor had been called, but she put this down to a high temperature. However, the boy insisted there had been a visitor who was most concerned about him, and who had spoken to him kindly. It seems that while he was ill Christopher had been visited by the ghost of the rectory. The large Elizabethan house was too big a place for just the rector and his family and it had been divided up into three flats. One of the residents, Mr George Spencer, had sensed a presence and an unnatural chill, and felt quite uncomfortable as a result, in the same room that Christopher had seen the ghost. It has been suggested the ghost was that of a priest but the identity of this shade remains a mystery. The rectory was demolished to widen the A60 road in the 1960s and it seems the ghost went with it.

Jim remembers being told stories of another Warsop ghost, that of the 'Man-in-the-Meadows'. The rectory meadows were between the A60 and Eastlands Lanes, but have now been built upon. Miners walking from Church Warsop to Welbeck colliery would use the meadows as a short-cut and they often talked of a man seen walking across the fields, especially in the early morning, who always gave a cheery greeting. No one seemed to know who this man was or why he should be about so early when not a miner himself. Talk amongst the miners suggested he was a ghost. One collier claimed he had met the 'Man-in-the-Meadows' one bright but damp summer's morning. After the man had greeted him and walked past, he turned to watch him go, noticing that, though he could clearly see his own footprints in the long, dewy grass, the stranger had left no trace. The figure in the meadows seemed harmless enough and to the Warsop miners the ghost became 'just one of those things'.

A clue to the possible identity of the ghost might be found in the sharp business acumen of Jim Rooke's grandfather. He had a grocery shop at the corner of Wood Street and had, by the arrangement of a special licence, the sole rights to supply bread and cheese to the prisoners being walked from the north of the county to the Crown Court at Nottingham. Was the 'Man-in-the-Meadows' the ghost of some executed prisoner retracing his last journey through Warsop to the gallows at Nottingham? In his fascinating book *Nottingham – A Place of Execution*, Terry Lambley recounts the sad events of several capital crimes in north Nottinghamshire. A likely candidate for the Warsop meadows ghost is Robert Powell, alias Harvey, of Worksop, who was executed for his part in a robbery of 40 guineas from the house of one John Leeming. Powell and an accomplice were both sentenced to death for the robbery. However, the accomplice was reprieved. Powell had used a pistol when resisting arrest and for this he suffered the full punishment of the law. Perhaps it is the aggrieved spirit of Robert Powell that wanders the fields near Warsop.

Ghostly Pilgrims

SOOKHOLM CHAPEL, near Warsop, is a site of ancient pilgrimage. The tiny church has some Anglo-Saxon features and has been a place of worship for over 1,000 years. It was near this spot that a local man met no less than twelve ghosts all at once. On a summer's night in 1925 a naturalist, a fellow of the Zoological Society, was out looking for owls. He had found owl pellets beneath an oak on his rambles during the day and had returned at night in the hope of seeing the birds hunting. He later recorded his experiences of that night for a local newspaper. His account, which has been paraphrased, tells the story: 'I was alone, pausing to fill my pipe. In the distance, dense woods, enfolded in an inky blackness, and silhouetted boldly against a blue-green sky. No sound, save the occasional hooting of a brown owl and, once, the shrill clamour of migrating birds passing overhead.

'For no reason at all my attention became fixed upon the middle of an open space. And, presently, the moonlight seemed to become more centralised, concentrating in a definite form. Quite distinctly now, before me stood a line of spectral figures, in concealing hoods and flowing robes. They were semi-transparent and diffused. I counted them, there were twelve. As I watched they arranged themselves, one behind the other, with their hands placed high on each other's shoulders. They then moved off in a silent, wavering motion. They moved across the moonlight space and vanished in the darkness.

'An optical illusion? A figment of my imagination? I think not. I am certain that I saw those twelve ghostly figures, and that they acted in the manner I've described. That which I have set down is not a dream. Perhaps I may visit that spot again in the hope of repeating that fascinating experience.'

This gentleman obviously feared that by telling his tale he risked being ridiculed, yet so strange was his experience that he felt he needed to share it. He related the story to a young lady of his acquaintance and her interest encouraged him to record it in writing. His account was published anonymously the following year.

The Seafaring Ghost at the Redbrick House

THE Redbrick House restaurant, two miles south of Warsop, on Forest Hill, offers a high standard of food and drink in the heart of Sherwood Forest. The house was built by Charles Jackson in 1844 and was originally called Prospect House, the name inspired by the view of the surrounding countryside that it commanded. Though the name was appropriate, Mr Jackson changed it to Forest Hill Lodge sometime between 1844 and his death on 3rd December 1861. The third son of Samuel and Mary Jackson, Charles is believed to have been a whaling captain, who, on making his fortune at sea, returned to his native Warsop. He is said to have been given the land on which to build the house by the Duke of Portland, in return for some undisclosed favour. The *County Directory* of 1844 records that Charles was a rich man in his own right; at the time of building his house he owned 80 acres of land.

Mr and Mrs Rippley became the owners in 1989. On the wall in the master bedroom are written the names of everyone that has lived at the house since it was built and Mr and Mrs Rippley added theirs to the list. Not long after their arrival, Mrs Rippley's father, Mr Robert Lightfoot, spoke of seeing a man in a long frock-coat standing by the front door. It seems that he had seen the same figure, outside the house, several times. Once when walking up the drive he met this man coming in the opposite direction, only to have him vanish from sight before he got to him. His dog, a Welsh springer spaniel, had also reacted to some unseen presence on the drive on several occasions.

With its hackles up and straining to slip the leash, the dog had displayed all the classic signs of having encountered a ghost. Mr Rippley was sceptical about his father-in-law's experiences – until he saw the ghost himself, that is.

One night in March 1990 Mr Rippley and some customers were enjoying a late night drink. From behind the bar his attention was attracted by a shadowy figure walking purposefully past the ground floor windows towards the door. However, nobody came in. His curiosity aroused as to the whereabouts of the caller, Mr Rippley immediately went outside. There was no trace of anyone in the grounds at all. Everyone present had seen the shape at the window and all were at a loss to account for it.

Mr Rippley had a new tarmac drive laid to the restaurant and whilst it was under construction he got his first good look at the ghost in broad daylight: 'I was driving up what remained of the old drive towards the house when I saw someone walking there. This was odd because we had tapes up to stop people going up there. At first I thought it was a woman, but then made out it was a man, clean-shaven, with long hair. He was wearing a long coat, the colour of a mac, with black gum boots on. I stopped the car and got out to see who it was, but he was gone. I walked round the house but there was no one there. The second time I was driving down the drive and he crossed in front of me, I got a good look at him, the same clothes and sort of unkempt looking. Again I stopped to find out who it was, but he had simply gone. I am not a believer, but I can tell you this is entirely genuine.'

The man in a long frock-coat has been seen at various times since, but always outside the house, on the drive and in the paddock. It would seem that Charles Jackson is still keeping an eye on his house.

WELBECK

The Abbey Tunnels

THE tunnels and underground rooms built by the 5th Duke of Portland were never intended to be a secret. The sheer scale of their construction and grandiose design made this an impossibility. The mystery that surrounds them is why they were built at all. There has been much speculation both at the time and since, but the most bizarre and notorious theory was revealed in the law courts in what has become known as the Druce-Portland case.

In his 1938 work, *A History of Welbeck Abbey and its Owners*, A. S. Turberville gives an unsensational description of the tunnels and their builder. Between 1869 and 1879 the Duke spent a vast amount of money, engaged a 'fleet of ponderous traction engines' and employed an army of thousands of masons, bricklayers, joiners, plumbers and navvies. The main tunnel is over 1,000 yards long, and is wide enough for several people to walk abreast. This tunnel leads from the house to the riding school, at one time second only in size to the famous Moscow Riding School. Parallel to this tunnel is a second, more roughly finished one, used by the workmen. Larger still is the tunnel from Welbeck to Worksop, over a mile and half long and wide enough for two carriages to pass through. This tunnel was intended to take the Duke's carriage unseen to Worksop station, where it could be driven straight onto a railway wagon for London, without its passenger having to leave it. As well as the tunnels there was a ballroom 160 ft long and 63 ft wide, and a library. Work continued on the excavation right up until the death of the Duke in 1879.

Quite naturally, there was rumour and speculation about the purpose of this vast undertaking. The Duke's habits were known to be eccentric; he often spent days alone in his apartments, receiving food through a hatch in the door. One rumour had it that the Duke was horribly scarred, another that he suffered some disfiguring disease.

However, in his preface Turberville states that, 'Many of the stories told about him are quite untrue; the description now given of his character and career. It is only just to his memory that the truth should be unravelled from the mass of foolish legend which has grown around his name.'

Turberville based his history on the Duke's own papers and the accounts left by those who knew him at first hand and seeks to redress the popular image of the Duke as an extreme eccentric: 'When he was a young man he lived a perfectly normal life, was a soldier, Member of Parliament for King's Lynn, and shewed much of his father's practical ability; but in later years he altogether retired from public life.'

As an 'official historian' to Welbeck Abbey it is not surprising that Turberville gives a polite account of the 5th Duke and his underground buildings. Nor is it surprising that he completely omits any mention of the famous Druce-Portland case. In 1896, some years after the death of the 5th Duke, a Mrs Druce pursued through the courts a claim on the Welbeck estates and title on behalf of her son. Such lawsuits were not uncommon. However, the claims made by Mrs Druce were quite remarkable. She said that her late husband, Mr Druce, a London grocer, was none other than the late Duke. It was her assertion that the late Duke had led a double life, travelling to London to assume the identity of Mr Druce the grocer, returning periodically to his ancestral home at Welbeck. As Mr Druce the Duke had successfully run a business and raised a family, but his true identity was revealed only to Mrs Druce herself. The tunnels, according to Mrs Druce, were constructed to allow the Duke to move between London and his country estate unseen. For eleven years, at a cost of thousands of pounds, this was the substance of the Druce-Portland case. Mrs Druce relentlessly pursued her claim, even after her son had died and at the expense of her own health. The matter was finally resolved in 1911, when her claim was rejected by the court once and for all.

Whatever the motives that led the Duke of Portland to build his underground structures, the subterranean passages of Welbeck are the most fabulous of all the tunnels of Sherwood: 'This feature of Welbeck is, indeed, like fairyland in its novelty and its inward comforts, and its adoption was a grand conception on the part of its noble owner' (Turberville p 438, quoting Jewitt and Hall, *The Stately Halls of England*, vol ii, p 347).

Welbeck Abbey is now a military college and on special occasions the tunnels are opened to visitors. The sense of wonder they inspire in all those who see them is tempered by a lingering sense of mystery; why were the tunnels built? Beyond philanthropic motives of providing work in hard times, beyond a desire for a lasting monument underground, could it be that the 5th Duke sought, by this extraordinary project, to leave future generations with an enigma, a profound mystery; and isn't this reason enough for the building of the tunnels of Welbeck?

WELLOW

Two Haunted Pubs

THE village takes its name from the Anglo-Saxon, meaning 'enclosure by the well or spring', and is famous today for its permanent maypole on the village green, one of only three in England. It would seem that few went thirsty in Wellow. The village once had five pubs, of which two remain, the Durham Ox and the Olde Red Lion, both of which are haunted. The other three, the White Horse, the Black Horse and the Live and Let Live are long gone. The village has also lost the ducking stool that once stood in Wellow Park.

In November 1977 a newspaper report appeared in the now defunct *Chronicle Advertiser* about the ghost at the Durham Ox. The then landlord, Mr Robert Renshaw, and his family had several experiences of the resident ghost. Phantom footsteps on the stairs were heard, and on one occasion Mrs Sandra Renshaw saw her daughter Stephanie sitting up in bed talking to some invisible companion. Stephanie, then aged six, insisted she was talking to 'the

little girl in the corner'. One night Mrs Renshaw was startled by the shade of a small woman or child in a grey cloak
brushing past her. She was so terrified by the apparition
that she let out a piercing scream that disturbed the whole
household. Mrs Renshaw may well have frightened the
ghost, for this was the last the family saw or heard of the
little grey lady. No one in the village could suggest a cause
for the haunting, but on the far side of the green, in the
Olde Red Lion, hangs an old framed photograph of the
maypole dancing, taken about 1930. In the midst of the
crowd is an extraordinarily small woman in a long coat. Is
this the living image of the ghost at the Durham Ox?

Dave and Julie Preston took on the pub in March 1990.
Through a catalogue of odd happenings they soon became
aware of the house's unusual tenant. Footsteps were heard
upstairs, when there was no one there. Customers and staff
would often stumble and fall up a short flight of stairs, as if
tripped. The hot water tap in the cellar switched itself on
and wasted gallons of water. Indeed, when Julie was reading the letter of enquiry I sent her to a member of the staff a
heavy brass plaque, bearing the legend 'Hands off the
Barmaid', inexplicably fell over, causing them both to jump.
The plaque had never fallen down before, nor has it since.

Just before opening time one evening Julie told me of
their strangest experiences: 'There has always been things
going on here. Glasses have moved on the shelves while
customers and staff have been watching them. Glasses fall
to the floor but don't break, odd things like that. But the
strangest thing happened just before we extended the dining area. This part of the pub was our downstairs living
room. Dave was in the habit of having a cup of tea here
after hours, maybe watching some TV before coming up to
bed. I was really ill, lying in bed upstairs. I heard the front
doors being shut and bolted. Just then something came to
the side of the bed. I thought to myself "please go and
fetch Dave, please fetch him", I was so ill. The shape
moved away. Well, by this time, Dave had come through to
the living room. Then something came down the stairs,
went past him and came round near the fireplace. He followed it across the room but it had vanished. He then shot
upstairs to me in bed, and found me very ill.'

Dave verified this: 'I saw something white come floating down the stairs. I just caught it out of the corner of my eye. It moved very fast and went into the other room. I took one quick look and ran straight upstairs. Something told me "go straight upstairs". I couldn't hear anything. I ran up and found Julie in a very distressed state. The ghost was leading me upstairs. My normal routine was to stay down here, but the ghost made me go up and it saved Julie's life. This was one of numerous incidents. We had some friends staying with us once, and we sat in this same room talking. Tony, one of our friends, needed an ashtray. I fetched one from the bar, a glass one. We had just started talking about the death of the husband of a mutual friend, when this ashtray simply exploded. It shattered, sending pieces of glass flying all over. There were pieces all around where Tony was sitting, all over the table under his seat, behind him, in the cushions of the chairs, everywhere. But not one piece hit Tony. It simply defies logic. Despite the breakages we are convinced that it is a friendly spirit.'

The family had a nanny staying with them during the summer of 1990. Her name was Mandy. On one occasion, her family were visiting her and were sitting in the down-stairs living room when a second ashtray shattered. As with the previous incident the ashtray was stationary on a table at the time, and no cause for it breaking could be found. Pint pots, used to hold pens to take orders for food, have also inexplicably shattered. The room where these incidents occurred has now become part of the main dining area. Guests could well be eating in the pub's most haunted spot.

Across the busy Newark road, on the edge of the village green, stands the Olde Red Lion, which dates from about 1600. It was originally a one-room inn with a row of farm labourers' cottages beyond; these were knocked through to extend the pub. The landlord of the Olde Red Lion is Mr John Henshaw. Incidents over the years have made John think the pub is haunted: 'Around about 6 o'clock one evening four people came into the pub. They ordered drinks and asked to see the menu. They had never been in the pub before, and there was no one else here except them. They sat down there, in that far corner there, for about 15 minutes. Suddenly they all got up and marched out. They never said a word, or said they were going or said "Good night". They just went, leaving half pints of beer. We like to think we sell beer that no one is going to leave. I felt quite upset, there was something they didn't like, I was really bothered by it.

'At about 8 o'clock that same evening the phone rang. It was the lady from the party that had got up and left. She said, "I'm phoning up to apologise for just walking out of your pub like that. Let me tell you there was nothing wrong with the pub. We were going to have a meal. We had to leave because I saw a figure in the middle of the room. He was sitting there, very hazy, but definitely a semi-transparent figure. I could make out that he wore boots, a flat cap, he was smoking a pipe and he had a dirty face. He was a little bloke, chubby, he looked like a coal miner or a chimney sweep that had come straight from work." She was concerned because people were walking through him. Only she could see him and it upset her. I said to her, "The man you're describing died five or six years ago, his name was Bill Davis."

'Well, Bill used to smoke a pipe, he used to prod it with his fingers and then cut tobacco with his knife. He always sat close to the fire, and as he got warm, he used to rub his forehead with his hands, and wipe the muck that he got from his pipe on his face. I'm very sceptical but what convinced me was her description. Bill was a lovely fellow. He used to sit and think for hours by the fire. If you can imagine 'The Archers', he was our Walter Gabriel. He used to tell lovely stories about his youth. Bill had been a stonemason who had worked at Rufford Abbey. He travelled all over the country, because stonemasons were few and far between. Although he had never married, he'd tell stories about the girls he'd known, and how many kids he'd got! Many people who remember Bill have said that if they saw him there now they wouldn't be frightened; he was that nice a guy. All I can say about this is that if he wants to be our ghost he's welcome.

'On another occasion we had a Nottingham lady come into the pub. She was a clairvoyant and told me there was a presence in the pub. I thought, I'm not falling for this and didn't tell her anything, I simply asked where. She said,

"You've got two, one in there right in the middle of the room." That was just where Billy used to sit, and there's no table there now. And the other she said is at the bottom of these stairs at the far end of the pub. I found out much later that a previous landlord had fallen down these stairs and been killed.'

John added that odd things occurred with one of the carver chairs in this room. After the chairs had been re-varnished one chair in particular showed signs of wear on one of the arms. Was this Bill, wearing away the varnish sitting in the same chair night after night?

The cellar at the Red Lion is directly behind the bar, beneath a simple trapdoor, and is about 5 ft high and 20 ft long. Its vaulted ceiling suggests great age, and the well at the far end appears to have been hewn out of the solid sandstone floor and is over 30 ft deep. The well could pre-date the present buildings and might be the original one from which the village took its name. According to John, a boy fell down this well and was drowned in the 1920s. It is said that every landlord of the Olde Red Lion since has seen the ghost of that boy. So far John has been lucky, he hasn't seen the ghost, but one day working alone in the cellar he did think his turn had come: 'At that time we had a bottling-up boy called Martin who was very light on his feet. Well this particular day I was down there and I turned to see this boy standing behind me. They nearly had to scrape me off the ceiling, I jumped that high! I frightened young Martin as well.'

Mr Tony Brown lived in the pub for over 40 years before retiring as landlord. He has also had strange experiences. 'I've seen one or two things. On one night in particular I woke in bed. To the left was a window, and the moon was shining through the curtains. I looked up towards the curtain and saw a shadow across the curtains. I thought my wife had got up and was looking out of the window. The shape came around the end of the bed, to my side of the bed and stood there looking at me. I said, "Whatever is the matter?" As soon I said that I realised that my wife was asleep next to me. I looked around again and the shape had gone. I lay there, I sweated a bit, but eventually I must have dropped off again.'

The Olde Red Lion is certainly thoroughly haunted, but as Mr Brown said, 'If you were a ghost where would **you** want to be?' The prospect of spending the afterlife in a fine country pub, with an everlasting pint, would surely appeal to many of us.

WORKSOP

The Mystery Tunnel of the Priory Gatehouse

FOR many years stories have circulated around Worksop of a tunnel leading from the Priory Gatehouse to Castle Hill, a distance of over two miles. Some old Worksopians I've spoken to insist on the tunnel's existence. Local tradition has it that the tunnel is now blocked off for safety reasons. Other local people dismiss the tunnel stories as wholly apocryphal. There are old drains and sewers in the town of ancient date, cut into the sandstone rock, which could be a source of the legend. However, to this day the question of the tunnel to Castle Hill remains a matter for speculation. In a letter to the local newspaper in June 1896, a resident of Retford (perhaps not the best place from which to attempt to advise Worksop folk) gave his explanation for the origins of the tunnel legend:

'Superstition and romanticism hang over all historic buildings, from the dungeon to the Minster; and, as an intermediate thing, the Worksop Priory Gatehouse has not escaped the daub of unreality. For many years it has been confidentially said that a secret passage connected the Castle Hill with the Gatehouse; and scores of people now living in the town believe in the existence of such an underground road. But I can assure them all that they are mistaken. There is no passage; not even the semblance of one. Some years ago, and before the Gatehouse was restored, the lads who went to the school saw, through an aperture in the wall, a dark hole in one part of the building. The little light that shone on this spot prevented anyone from concluding what the mysterious hole really was, and with what it was connected. Conjectures were made, and the romantic minds of the schoolboys imagined all sorts of things. They threw stones into the opening; fathomed it with poles. Some of them, bolder than the rest, did not stop here; they entered the chasm with marvellous intrepidity, and, for a while, were lost from sight. Being of a theatrical turn of mind, they, on their emerging from the darkness, told soul stirring stories of their unseen adventures, and swore they had walked, at least, 200 yards up a dank passage, "black as Erebus and old night". Their comrades wonderingly believed them, and scattered about the daring deeds that had been done in their midst. The idea got rotted in the boyish mind – they had faith in the narrations of the brave explorers – nothing could persuade them that a tunnel-like opening did not exist – things were magnified, as they usually are, and ultimately rumour and popular belief had it that from the old Priory Gatehouse to the Castle Hill ran an unilluminated subterranean passage that had been utilised by the Black Canons of the old time. I, myself, have been over the whole building within the last three months; and dare I say that there is not the slightest trace of any such passage. Contrarily, the walls are all solid, the only exits being the doors and windows. I trust this will suit your correspondent. W. R. D. (Retford)'

This would seem to settle the matter. However, one life-long Worksop resident recalls that his father was engaged in the construction of Avenue Road, Worksop, between the wars, and that the necessary excavations revealed a tunnel running from the Gatehouse in the direction of Castle Hill. His father told him of the several tons of hardcore needed to fill the tunnel to allow the work to continue. More myth-making? Despite the lack of evidence the stories of the Worksop tunnel persist. Caves, caverns and tunnels have a special place in our folklore. In many traditional stories they are the realm of the fairy folk, dwarfs and cobalts. Tunnel myths such as Worksop's occur all over the British Isles and are often connected to churches.

A Travelling Companion

OUR roads and highways are some of the landscape's oldest features. Not surprisingly, then, a host of myths and legends have become attached to them down through the ages. The following is a 'phantom hitchhiker' story, variations of which can be found throughout the country.

It was mid-afternoon in early autumn at the turn of the century. A young army officer in a borrowed dogcart was travelling towards Worksop. At a bend in the road the soldier saw the figure of a tramp, standing as if waiting for someone. So wretched was the appearance of the unfortunate fellow that the young man drew up the cart alongside him, and offered a lift to town. The soldier noticed the pallor of the man's face, made all the more striking by a bright red muffler spotted with green, worn around the neck.

The young man was not at all put out by the tramp's silent acceptance of the offer. Sensing conversation to be unwelcome, he watched as the man climbed aboard. As the cart rattled through the woods the despondency of his silent passenger seemed to seep into the marrow of his bones, and the soldier resolved to do something to ease the poor fellow's plight. Though the afternoon was bright and clear the dank autumnal smell of decay in the air quelled all cheerful feeling. The pony was brought to a swift trot to bring this now melancholic journey to an early conclusion.

Entering the town and turning into the yard of the Ship Inn, the soldier called for the ostler. The old servant was instructed to tend the pony and give the ailing passenger aboard the cart a hot meal. The ostler looked puzzled, and said, 'Yes sir, but what passenger would that be?' Turning around, the soldier saw his travelling companion was gone. 'Well I hope he didn't fall off! I never heard him get down. If he turns up feed him at my expense. He's a rather miserable looking fellow with a red scarf around his neck.'

As he said this a waiter standing in the doorway stepped forward. 'I heard you describe the tramp, sir, and I want you to see what is in here.'

Going through the inn and behind the bar they entered into a small room. There lay the corpse of the tramp, red muffler livid against the blue throat. 'That's the man I picked up on the road just now!' exclaimed the soldier. The waiter then gravely told him the corpse had lain there since 4 pm the previous day, awaiting the coroner's enquiries. It became apparent that the soldier had picked up his passenger at the very spot where the body was found, and at the very same hour.

'I am the Spirit of Dark and Deadly Waters'

NEAR Worksop's ancient Priory church flows a stretch of water known as the Canch. It runs through the park and the Canch walk is a pleasant spot for a stroll, at least during the day. At night the overhanging trees and inky waters present a different prospect. Those who use Canch walk as a short cut to the Priory car park after dark, do not, understandably, linger there. If they were to become acquainted with the Canch's resident ghost they could be forgiven for always taking the long way round.

In January 1906, in the local newspaper, an account was given by someone who met the Canch ghost: 'It was about 11 pm when I was by Mr Bramer's mill. It was moonlit but cloudy, and there was a frost on the ground. I stopped for a moment and leaned over the rail to see whether the Canch had begun to freeze over or not. Starting to walk again I saw a figure clothed in grey coming towards me from the direction of Church Walk. It looked like a woman and I wondered what she thought about my leaning over the rail. As we approached I saw she seemed to have a shawl over her head and face, and I suddenly realised that, as she walked, her footsteps made no sound, whereas mine clomped on the hard ground. I thought there was something weird about her and I felt all of a tingle. We continued to approach, and when within three yards of her I looked up to see her face, at that moment she vanished. I hurried home and told my father what I'd seen, he told me to tell the paper, as if it is anybody playing a joke it ought to be shown up.'

The paper reported that some years earlier a woman's body had been pulled from the Canch after lying in the waters for a fortnight. Other sightings of the Canch ghost suggest the figure to be that of a monk. The fields around the Canch were watermeadows belonging to the Priory. However, the Augustinian friars of Worksop Priory wore black, not grey, habits so the identity of the Canch ghost remains a mystery.

This is not the only ghost in that part of Worksop. The Canch runs past the Priory churchyard, reputedly haunted by 'The Blue Lady'. She is said to walk the path between the 12th-century gatehouse and the church. She has been seen sitting on an oddly shaped branch, set at a right angle to the trunk, of one of the trees that line the path. Though these trees are far from contemporary to the gatehouse this branch, immediately discernible to the casual observer, would provide a very apt resting place for a spirit doomed to walk the path for all eternity.

Joe White's Ghost

A horse trader, pig breeder and scrap metal merchant with 'sundry other vocations', Joe White was a real Victorian 'character'. Though he could hardly read or write, he was a master trader, in anything from which a ready profit could be made. It was said that Joe was seen in the capitals of Europe on business. Foreign travel was a rare thing in those days, even for the gentry, but perhaps Joe's gypsy connections gave him the 'wanderlust'. He and his family lived in Sandhill Cottage, Worksop. Nearby, on a patch of ground known as 'Joe White's Piece', gypsies would come and encamp and trade. A generous man, he once arranged a supper at the Sherwood Inn for 70 of his out of work friends. Joe is still talked about in Worksop; but it is for the weird events, as first reported in the *Retford and Gainsborough Times* in March 1883, that he is most remembered.

On the evening of Wednesday, 21st February 1883 Mrs White was washing up at the kitchen table by candlelight. Suddenly the table inexplicably lifted itself up at one end, shrugging off the dishes and the candle. Mrs White caught the dishes but was plunged into darkness as the candle hit the floor. Recovering from her shock, she relit the candle but could find no explanation for her startling experience. Rather than frighten the children she dismissed the incident and put it down to 'one of those things'.

The following week, on Monday, 26th February, Mr White went away on business and Mrs White invited a girl called Eliza Rose to come and stay with her and the children during his absence. Rose, as she was known, was an unhappy teenager with a troubled background and she readily accepted the kind offer. Uncle Tom, Joe's brother, was the only other adult staying at the house. Nothing unusual occurred all that week until Thursday night. Mrs White and Rose had sat up late talking in the kitchen, while Uncle Tom and the children were asleep upstairs. They were abruptly disturbed by the sound of something falling down the stairs. Rushing out of the room, they were astonished to see several kitchen utensils tumbling down the stairs, followed by a burning piece of coal. No one else was near the stairs or the landing. The noise of the falling objects and alarmed cries of the ladies woke those upstairs and they emerged from the bedrooms. All denied being responsible for what was obviously a dangerous prank. Mr White returned home the following day, Friday. He listened to accounts of the previous night's happenings but wouldn't entertain the idea of a supernatural cause. He was soon to change his mind.

At about 1.30 in the afternoon a rain of objects, knives, forks, pots and pans that had all previously been in the kitchen, cascaded down the stairs. This was followed by china ornaments flying through the downstairs rooms and smashing themselves against the walls, one narrowly missing Mr White's head. Footsteps were heard around the house where nobody was present. Regretting his earlier belittling of the ladies' experience, Mr White called for a policeman. PC Higgs soon arrived and, with several neighbours, witnessed the inexplicable phenomenon. The constable watched as a glass jar flew out of a cupboard, through the house and out into the yard where it smashed, followed by a drinking glass which rose up from a chest of drawers.

Similar occurrences continued until two o'clock in the morning, resuming again at 8 am the next day. A treasured grandfather clock, which hadn't worked for over a year, struck the hour and crashed to the floor. A heavy iron bedstead moved of its own accord and a chest of drawers was completely smashed. 'Joe White's ghost', far from being a 'playful spirit', threatened the very fabric of the family home.

The wanton destruction continued all that Saturday. No physical cause could be found at all. By now PC Higgs was busy keeping the gathering crowd of onlookers away from the house and out of range of the flying crockery, cutlery and furniture coming from it. That afternoon a lady from the Salvation Army called at the house. In his statement to Frank Podmore of the Society for Psychical Research, given on 8th April, Joe told what happened: 'At about 2 pm a Salvation Army woman came in and was talking to me as I lay on the squab; she stood near the inner door; Rose was near the outer door, having bought some carpet. There were two candlesticks on the bin, at the end near the fireplace. Suddenly something dropped behind the Salvation Army woman. No one saw it go through the air; but we turned around and found that it was one of the brass candlesticks. It was balanced on the small end where the candle goes, and was wobbling about at the end. Then the Salvation woman said "I must go," and she went.'

By four o'clock in the afternoon Joe was at the end of his tether. Though she had done nothing herself, Joe had become convinced that Rose was the root cause of the tempest gripping his family home. Later in his statement to Frank Podmore Joe said: 'A lamp glass had fallen several times without breaking; but at last that fell and broke. Then an empty bottle flew off from the mantelpiece. That was one of the last things that happened. Well then, I couldn't stand it any longer. Wherever the lass seemed to go, things seemed to fly about. So I said to her, "You'll have to go". She began to roar, but my wife gave her some tea and she went. That was between 4 and 5 pm, very soon after the last disturbance. Nothing happened after she left. We sat up in the kitchen that night, a lot of us, as the newspapers tell; but nothing happened at all.'

Frank Podmore was dispatched to Worksop by the SPR when the case reached the national papers. He arrived in

Worksop on Saturday, 7th April 1883. His detailed description of the house and its history and the thorough witness statements he gathered from all those involved were published in volume 12 of the *Proceedings of the Society for Psychical Research, 1896–97*. In his general conclusion Podmore sums up his opinions on Joe White's ghost: '. . . it is hard to conceive by what mechanical appliances, under the circumstances described, the movements could have been effected. The clock for instance – a heavy American one – thrust out from the wall in a horizontal direction, so as apparently to clear a 4 foot bedstead that lay immediately beneath it, and the nail from which it was suspended remained in the wall. The objects thrown about in the kitchen moved generally, but by no means always, in the direction of the outer door. And it is noticeable that, in most cases, they do not appear to have been thrown, but in some manner borne or wafted across the room; for, though they fell on a stone floor, fifteen or sixteen feet distant, they were often unbroken, and were rarely shivered. And it is impossible to reconcile the account given of the movement of some other objects, variously described as "jerky", "twirling" and "turning over and over", with the supposition that the objects depended on any fixed support or were in any way suspended.

'Lastly, to suppose that these various objects were all moved by mechanical contrivances argues incredible stupidity, amounting almost to imbecility, on the part of all the persons who were not in the plot.'

Joe White was left to count the cost and Mrs White to clear up the mess. Trickery has been suggested – Joe was a well-known prankster about the town – but the poltergeist had wreaked havoc. Joe would have been out of pocket from the whole affair, indeed all the bacon that hung curing in the house is said to have gone off. He was certainly justified in ordering Rose from the house as all the activity stopped once she had left. The presence of the troubled girl does suggest a classic poltergeist episode. It has been suggested by researchers that emotional turmoil, especially in teenagers, can manifest itself in just such telekinetic vandalism as was seen in this case. However, the initial incident, that of Mrs White's washing up being tipped from the table, occurred before Rose entered the house. All we know for certain is that once Rose left there were no further disturbances from Joe White's ghost.

BIBLIOGRAPHY

D. J. Bradbury, *Ollerton B.C. – Before the Colliery*. Wheel Publications, 1985

D. J. Bradbury, *W'dhus and the Wolf-hunters*. Wheel Publications, 1989

Brand's *Antiquities*. 1813

Cornelius Brown (Ed), *Notes about Notts*. 1874

S. Jackson Coleman, *Quaint Lore of Nottinghamshire*. Folklore Fellowship, London

Richard de Vries, *On the Trail of Robin Hood*. Crossbow Books, 1982

Peter Beresford Ellis, *Celt and Saxon – the Struggle for Britain AD 410–937*

Sir James G. Frazer OM, *The Golden Bough; A Study in Magic and Religion*. Macmillan and Co, Abridged Edition 1950

H. Garbett, *Brief History of Shireoaks*. Century Brochure, St Lukes Parish Church, 1961

William Harrod, *The History of Mansfield and its Environs*. 1801

David Hool, *The Tales of Robin Hood*. Notts. County Council, 1983

Polly Howat, *Tales of Old Nottinghamshire*. Countryside Books, 1991

Washington Irving, *Abbotsford and Newstead Abbey*

Dom David Knowles, *The Religious Orders in England*

Terry Lambley, *Nottingham – A Place of Execution from 1201 to 1929*

Jim Lees, *The Legendary Exploits of Robin Hood in the City of Nottingham*. Temple Nostalgia Press, 1987

Robert Mellors, *In And About Nottinghamshire*

Frank Moody, *My Lifetime of Memories of Laxton*

Capt Roy Peters *Ancient Bassetlaw*. North Trent Publishing, Sutton-in-Ashfield, 1990 and *Whitwell and Barlborough*

Ken Radford, *Tales of Witchcraft and Sorcery*

A. S. Turberville, *A History of Welbeck Abbey and its Owners*. 1938

Robert Thoroton, *History of Nottinghamshire*

INDEX